therapist to have set up couch in Britain since Sigmund Freud'.
She lives in London and lectures extensively worldwide.

Also by Susie Orbach

Bodies
On Eating
The Impossibility of Sex
Towards Emotional Literacy
What's Really Going on Here
Fat is a Feminist Issue
Fat is a Feminist Issue II
Hunger Strike

Also by Susie Orbach and Luise Eichenbaum

Bittersweet: Love, Competition & Envy in Women's Relationships
What Do Women Want? Exploding the Myth of Dependency
Understanding Women: A Feminist Psychanalytic Approach
Outside In Inside Out: A Feminist and Psychoanalytical Approach
to Women's Psychology

Also by Susie Orbach, Lisa Appignanesi and Rachel Holmes

Fifty Shades of Feminism

In Therapy

How conversations with psychotherapists
really work

Susie Orbach

PROFILE BOOKS

First published in Great Britain in 2016 by
PROFILE BOOKS LTD
3 Holford Yard
Bevin Way
London WC1X 9HD
www.profilebooks.com

By arrangement with the BBC
The BBC Radio 4 logo is a trade mark of the British
Broadcasting Corporation and is used under licence.

1 3 5 7 9 10 8 6 4 2

Typeset in Photina by MacGuru Ltd

Printed and bound by CPI Group (UK) Ltd, Croydon, CR0 4YY

The moral right of the author has been asserted.

A CIP catalogue record for this book is available from the British Library.

ISBN 978 1 78125 753 1
eISBN 978 1 78283 311 6

For Jeanette Winterson, who has always wanted
to know what goes on in the consulting room

Contents

Preface

Welcome to the consulting room. What follows is a play script – the verbatim notes of therapy sessions, initially made for the radio, with the addition of my commentary about what I was thinking and feeling during the making of them. I also include some general observations about psychological and social phenomena.

Writing about clinical work and what actually occurs in the therapy is hampered by the confidentiality of the therapy relationship. It makes transcripts of actual sessions all nigh impossible. I have tried to solve the problem of how to invite the reader into the feel of what occurs by using actors to give a sense of the taste and flavour of an encounter. The therapy encounter defies conventional back and forth conversation as it searches to meet the hurts and burdens of the one who is seeking help.

The play script that has emerged conveys the feel of the consulting room. These encounters were not in any way scripted. They are the embodiment of what the characters expressed; characters who come to the therapy in search of understanding and relief from their anguish, confusions and problems.

Therapists don't so much solve such issues as attempt to open up new doors – emotional, intellectual, physical – for the individual, couple or family, to expand their notions of the roots and interplay of their difficulties so that they can intervene with themselves and with others differently. By listening intently to the narrative and the feelings, and hearing the contradictions that are felt by the individual, therapy tries to situate the person as an agent who can become interested in why she or he acts and feels the way they do and how they can develop a growing emotional complexity.

Like literature, psychoanalysis reveals the commonality of human experience by drilling into the particularities of the individual. The way an individual imagines and projects, the way the individual reads and misreads situations speaks to us in our own private struggles. A highly personal and specific story unfolds to reveal common human themes. Consider the man who disavows his girlfriend when in public but has no difficulty being privately intimate. The woman feels hurt and insecure. She becomes tongue-tied and disappears into herself as though indeed she does not exist for him. She sits waiting to be rescued. Taking this a step deeper, we discover that the man is acutely anxious although he is not aware of it. Greeting friends at a bar is a performance for him, not an easy pleasure. He steals himself to do it. He was brought up to play the piano in public from an early age – a talent he has since foregone – and learned the tricks of being on show. But it cost him emotionally. He felt unprotected going into public, wanted to hold his mother or father's hand, but came to feel ashamed of his need. He drops his girlfriend, like he felt dropped, and armours himself in performance mode. His girlfriend carries his insecurity for him and it has a salience for her because growing up she felt her mother's attention desert her when her much elder brother, father and grandfather came home from work. She's accustomed to being dropped yet finds its unbearable. Her shame about wanting to be included seals her mouth. She can't find a way in with her boyfriend just as she couldn't at dinner time with her father, grandfather and brother. Her intimate relationship with her boyfriend is hidden as was her closeness with her mother.

The emotional trope this couple share is confusion about dependency and need. They enact their disappointments with each other. As we unpick what drives each of their behaviours we come across the human search for secure attachment and recognition and the ways in which that search becomes derailed. We know about this. It's why we cry at the movies when the lovers come together. We understand that longing. We feel that longing. We may crave that belonging. The specific tells the general. And so it is with psychotherapy. Each story tells us about the individual or the couple while it tells us about ourselves. We want to know about others' struggles because we want to know more deeply about ourselves and the project of being human.

The Making of the Programme

This is not a text book. My aim in making the programmes out of which this book came was to get as near to the experience of the consulting room as I could. In previous books, *Fat is a Feminist Issue*, *Understanding Women*, *What Do Women Want*, *Bittersweet* and *Bodies*, I wrote about what I was discovering about longings, conflicts, and confusions and used vignettes to describe and theorise the process of therapy and the theory that Luise Eichenbaum and I were developing.

In *The Impossibility of Sex*, I wrote a set of imaginary cases told from the point of view of a fictionalised version of myself. I wanted to convey the craft of the working therapist breathing, sweating, challenged, while thinking and feeling her patient's dilemmas. Kevin Dawson, the Producer, had read it, pitched it to the BBC and they offered us a series of 15-minute programmes for BBC Radio 4 about the process of therapy. I knew I didn't want to script something; that would not show how therapy actually goes. I had recently done a couple of mini therapy type sessions with actors in a Wallace Shawn play directed by Ian Rickson. They and a series of sessions done earlier with Kate Bland for Cast Iron Radio and for an initiative by Jordan McKenzie for The Gay Men's Choir, had taken the therapy out of the consulting room without abandoning the conventions of the therapeutic session. I knew Ian's genius with actors (we had occasionally worked together in the rehearsal room over the years when he was doing a new production) and I hoped that he would be able to choose and prepare actors to take part in a series in which they become characters who are in therapy with me.

The three of us met for what was to be a first for all of us. Kevin had little knowledge of therapy but knew how to produce, Ian could choose actors who were strong on improvisation and I had to stay as true to my craft as I could with the wrinkle that I would pretend to know the people coming to talk with me in my consulting room.

People who have listened to the radio programmes have imagined that I carefully drew out a list of specifications for the characters. Not so. That wouldn't have felt real to me. People are always more surprising and layered than a description can be and the unfolding of that is one of the great joys for therapists in the consulting room. I suggested very little to Kevin and Ian in our meetings beyond the barest of outlines. I said I wanted to see a couple whose difficulties might be linked to patterns in their parent's relationships. I suggested a woman in her forties who might have emigrated early on in her life. A 60-year-old trade unionist whose second marriage had broken down and who was feeling desperate. A young woman in her late twenties or early thirties who appeared to have everything but felt nothing. A first session with someone whose work life had not panned out.

From these rudiments, chosen for no particular reason except to give the range of a therapist's working day (although less various than a working week's practice), Kevin and Ian worked up a backstory which they then brought to me to check for authenticity. I knew that pretty much whatever they came up with would be alright because fiction, while less dense than the facts of an ordinary life, can nevertheless show so much more about a life than a simple narration in non-fiction. Thus I wasn't worried about authenticity. I knew it would or could be.

With barely three agreed sentences on each character, Ian worked with the actors to embody and grow these personae. I was reluctant to use actors whose voices were familiar on radio as I didn't want to draw the listeners' attention away from the therapy process. When Liz White playing Louise walked in to do the couples session, I had a faint sense of recognition. Later, I realised it was she who was giving birth in *Call the Midwife* the night before on TV. Peter Wright playing John is an actor with tremendous presence who I'd seen on stage several times but in roles with enough variety that I couldn't quite place him, and that was a guide. Noma Dumezweni had not yet been cast in Harry Potter, and Noo Kirby playing Harriet, Nat Martello White playing Richard and Sinead Matthews playing Jo were highly accomplished on the stage too, thus known to a smaller not radio audience. All six are superb actors but not so starry that the audience would be focused on their other roles or personalities.

The set-up to record was clean and simple. Perhaps not so from the Sound Engineer, Gareth Isles', point of view. I wore an unobtrusive wireless lapel mike as did my 'patient', we recorded in my consulting room, with me sitting in the same chair as I habitually do, and two rooms away, Gareth created an extensive recording studio. Kevin wanted to ensure the sound would be good enough to pick up nuances of breath, sighs, tears or whatever was to emerge.

Before the session started, when the actor was being miked up and getting a final prep from Ian at a local Café Nero, Kevin and I would talk about who was coming to see me that hour. I tried to familiarise myself with their backstory from a paragraph that Ian had given me.

The doorbell rings, and the person comes up the stairs and is instructed to walk into my room – save for Sinead Matthews who is playing Jo and needs to be shown where to go. I greet and welcome them. There they find two large beige leather chairs, a brown leather sofa with blue cushions, a blue Caucasian rug by a large window overlooking a garden, and many, many books.

They sit on the sofa and talk, or not, as would be the case in any session, and then at about the twenty or twenty-five-minute level, the length of half a session, I bring it to an end. We both walk out of the consulting room and into the ersatz studio where Ian, Kevin and Gareth are sitting with cans on their heads.

We debrief, the actor goes off and we do the next session.

In the following week, having listened to the recording and

worked out how to edit down to the prerequisite 15-minute broadcast in a way that retains the integrity of the session including the pauses, we meet to do finer cuts and voice-over. Therapy is not entertainment, like a mini radio play or serial whose conventions we have absorbed. It can crackle with intensity but it can be laboured or sound incoherent. We wanted to keep the feel of all of that and I believe we did.

Therapy has its own dramas. We make different kinds of patterns and linkages in the therapy room. Sometimes there will be a startling interpretation which will thrill a radio audience by its unexpected capacity to change the direction of how someone feels and perceives things. Equally, listening into therapy would turn out to be quite unusual radio. The individual is looking for the words she wants to say, the patterns that need to be made or the emotions that need to be undammed. It's not neat and it doesn't follow a straightforward narrative. In any given session insight might happen but sometimes the job of the therapist is to sit and hear and absorb and make oneself available for moments of connection. It can be anti-drama. The focus when cutting the programmes was to be faithful enough to the process of therapy.

I didn't set out in this series to show what happens when misunderstandings occur but of course they are inevitable. Therapy will sometimes engender misunderstanding and when this occurs, the therapist tries to address it. We use the therapy relationship a bit like a laboratory. When something goes amiss between therapist and client or words or intentions of either's are misinterpreted, that becomes part of the work of therapy. We call this process an enactment and in the sessions, we see several examples of this, most notably with Jo. The question then became, how to keep enough of the 'enactment' in the programme so the listener might understand how the therapist deals with it.

From rough cuts, we went into a studio to do a series of explanatory voice-overs. Kevin wanted these outside of the therapy room and in a studio in order to create a different soundscape. These were conducted in a conversational way and spliced in. Ian's genius was to prep the actors, but in doing so, he was of course having to think about how to direct me, without appearing to. I am not an actor. In talking about it subsequently he said he did so by ramping up the number of tricky things the improvisations would throw at me so that I was in a heightened state. In this way he created mini psychological conundrums for me to respond to.

Despite the artifice, these mini sessions convey the flavour and feel of the therapy room. Together the three of us and the individual actors had found a way to mimic the aesthetic arc that would end up on the radio.

Richard and Louise

This is Richard and Louise's fourth session. Louise is from the Hull and Richard is first-generation London-born whose mother came from the Caribbean. He's a compact man, 5 foot 7 inches, with striking dreadlocks, leather jacket and trainers. Louise is the same height. She wears combat boots and a long skirt. Her hair is flowy and lush. They are in their early thirties. Louise is about to have a baby and things have become frayed during the pregnancy.

We can hear the tension in their relationship as they climb the stairs. He's coming as Richard; she reminds him he is coming as part of a couple – Richard AND Louise. The session usually starts with a skirmish.

Louise Hi.

Richard Hi Susie.

Susie Hi, come on in.

Richard Right.

Louise Nice to see ya. Um, see, yeah, well we've got to make sure that we leave on time because we are parked in a really dodgy spot.

Richard It will be alright, it will be alright.

Louise   It probably won't be alright but as long as we leave on time, then we have got more chance.

Louise is trying to draw me into a conversation about Richard and what she experiences as a certain kind of casualness or neglect, in this instance, about risking a parking fine. He, for his part, is trying to shush her up. This is the pattern they've shown in the previous sessions.

Susie   OK.

Richard   Relax.

Louise   *Laugh.*

Susie   I'm sorry, I'm not quite getting what's going on between you, or maybe I am!

Richard   No, I just keep telling her to relax, you know, she is just always on at me – things like the car, I just feel like, you know, she's on my case. I am constantly under attack.

Susie   Do you think that you might default to feeling under attack and that in this instance it might be more that Louise is nervous?

Louise   I *am* nervous. I am nervous about money, about time. I think these are the essential problems. I am really aware of the fact that I am eight months pregnant and about to have a baby. In one week's time I will be full term, so the baby could be born then, and yet you haven't been to a nursery shop with me, you haven't bought anything for the baby with me, all your plans are about time out of the house, and it is making me really nervous.

Susie　I think it might help if you, Louise, said 'I feel' instead of 'you do'. That way Richard might be able to hear what's troubling you a little more easily.

Louise　I feel like you are leaving everything to me, I feel quite lonely when I am walking around picking things for our baby.

Richard　Well, you never walk so I don't know what you are talking about, you never walk do you.

Louise　*Laugh.* I never walk!

Richard　You never walk anywhere, you just sit at home all the time.

Louise　That is a ridiculous thing to say. When I go shopping – I don't do it online, I go to a shop and I walk around the shop, that is what I am talking about.

Richard　Yeah, because Mum helps her pick up all the stuff doesn't she, Mum's always there to help you out.

Louise　I am not having a baby with your mother, I am having a baby with you, Rich.

And actually, I don't know which is the better prospect. *Laugh.*

Richard　Why are you making comments like that? Wh… wh… what is it, what is the thing with my mum? All she wants to do is help out, make sure that you are not lonely while I am out there working hard trying to make sure that we keep the wolf away from the door, and you are ridiculing my mum, what is all that about?

Louise   I am not ridiculing your mum. I'm just saying that I want to make these decisions with *you*, I am having a baby with *you*, not your mum, she is not your substitute and you shouldn't see her that way.

Richard   Alright, alright.

When you are with a couple they demonstrate how their relationship is and the ways they interact. It can be quite delicate to work out how long to let a dispute run. It might be that their style is to fight and come to a resolution. It might be that fighting creates distance from one another. It might be that fighting heightens their passion. Or it might be that being criticised and feeling beleaguered is a pattern they've imbibed from their parent's relationship or how they were treated. There are so many possibilities when a couple is in the room together that I need to watch it for long enough to know the emotional spaces that each one of them occupies and what they psychologically carry for each other.

Listening to them zigzagging it is hard for Louise's point – at least so far – to be heard by Richard. He gets busy pushing her off course by criticising her. In one way it is simple: you're nagging and hassling me so I'm going to get back at you. Inevitably, the more she pushes, the further he backs away or appears obtuse.

Richard appears very laid-back and Louise rather systematic about what's not right and what needs attending to. She's sitting forward intently and he's put himself in the far corner of the sofa, legs spread, quasi-relaxed, quasi-dismissive. Their embodiment mirrors character traits which have psychological significance for them as a couple and each other as individuals. Richard relies on Louise's lists and scolding. He's been responsible from a very early age and very conscientious about earning. He wants to be free of responsibilities that aren't to do with money. Her remonstrations keep him aware of the other things he needs to be doing. She carries his list in her head like an outsourced memory stick.

Louise has always loved Richard's more laid-back attitude. Until the middle of her pregnancy, she bathed in it and was able to relax with him. The change has been hard for her as she can't use the laid-back part now for herself. It feels too irresponsible.

Observing how they divide up their psychological ways of being leads to the question of how the therapist can intervene to reshape those places which they once valued in each other but which aren't working now. My job is to help them walk alongside each other, to amplify their voices to each other so that they can hear one another, rather than be alternately bounced on a seesaw of: you're the baddy, no you're the baddy.

Susie   We talked last week about how hard it is for you to imagine being a dad. You are giving Louise your mum rather than giving her yourself. Maybe it will be very different when the baby arrives, but I sense that up to now it feels like it is just a scary proposition.

Richard Yeah, I guess I have been thinking about my dad.

Susie Uh-huh.

Richard I mean yeah, but I am not going to be like him, I mean I'm not going to disappear like he disappeared.

Louise Richard, you already *are*. You're not around. You haven't been around.

Like, I find it difficult, I find things difficult, I can't even reach my boots to zip them up at the moment cos my stomach's in the way. God knows how fat people cope. But you don't help me do these little things.

Susie So in other words, Louise, the caring that you used to experience and must have been part of the reason you wanted to have a family together, has disappeared. And Richard, you may not be aware that you would spontaneously go towards looking after and looking out for Louise.

Louise That's exactly it.

Richard Yeah, maybe.

Louise It's like …

Susie Sshhh, let him think.

I have the sense that Louise's understandable grievances are crowding Richard. She sees it as him running away but for him to reflect on what she is upset about, Louise needs to back off. Otherwise we are in a psychological cha-cha routine where he retreats, she chases or criticises, and he retreats further. This maintains the same distance between them rather than the beginning of a coming together.

Richard   Yeah, I mean the dynamic's changed, it feels like some of the fun, some of the fun's gone, you know, it's – I thought having a kid was meant to be fun you know, and we're meant to be, you know, celebrating this journey, but the vibes I am picking up all the time just feel passive-aggressive.

Susie   What about your own vibe inside, Richard? Do you think it's possible that you might be quite a bit more scared than you know, than you acknowledge to yourself?

When working with a couple you can see the projections they foist on each other. He's making the problems all about her and she's making them all about him. By asking him to listen to his own vibe I'm hoping to move him from a defensive attacking and rather dismissive position to see what feelings and fears he is dismissing inside of himself.

Richard   Oh yeah.

Louise   What are you scared of?

Richard   I guess how I'll mess it up.

Louise   *Laugh.*

And as she laughs she herself becomes dismissive of his fears. She doesn't want to know about them any more than he does.

Richard   Well …

Louise   Yeah but you haven't even started yet, you haven't even …

Richard   Yeah but you know it's like you kinda – you know …

Maybe I am more like my dad than I realise maybe. Maybe the feelings I am having right now are the feelings that he was having. Maybe.

Susie   Uh-huh.

Richard   You know, these feelings of destruction that I have, you know sometimes I just want to tear the place down.

Louise   Oh my God. *Laugh.*

Richard   I do, I just feel like smashing the place up.

Susie   Louise, if Richard's telling you what he is feeling, this is so the two of you can connect rather than for you to jump on him.

Richard is showing his fear. This terrifies him. It terrifies Louise but if both of them can bear it, she will know him better, he will know himself (at this moment) better and it will bring them closer. It will redraw and deepen the emotional field between them.

It sounds like a simple thing to do but it is a psychological shift for both of them to hear and bear. The fear is a fear he is anxious about. It is not inevitable that he is or will be like his disappearing father. It is not a reality. It is a worry.

Encountering fear doesn't make it bigger or more real. Curiously, it can make it more manageable. Its shape can change and become porous and less monolithic. It's worth engaging with because it will move them into a different and deeper relationship to each other.

Louise for her part will have to expand her view of Richard. She will have to see his vulnerability. If Louise can hear his fears rather than rubbish them, she will add to his capacity to examine and know them. If he can acknowledge his vulnerability, which he is starting to do by expressing himself, he can begin the process of accepting it in himself, aided by her understanding.

Louise   Yeah but it is pretty frightening to hear that you would want to tear the place down.

Richard   Well that's how I feel.

Susie   What interests me is that when Richard showed you a bit of his vulnerability, Louise, you kind of pooh-poohed it, pushed it away or it wasn't good enough.

You are wanting more closeness, Louise, and part of getting there may be accepting where he is at and where you are at.

Louise   I just feel really far away from him, from, from you.

Richard   Alright, alright, but you know, I'm here, you know I'm

11

	looking out for us, I am not going to run away am I? The closer we get, I'll get the lads, I'll get the Poles to take over the workload and I will be with you, and mum will be there as well.
Louise	I don't want your mum there, I'm sorry.
Richard	Why don't you want my mum there?
Louise	Because she is not my mum. I don't want your mum at my birth, I don't.
Richard	Why don't you want her at the birth?
Louise	I don't want your mum looking at my vagina quite frankly.
Richard	What's all that about?
Louise	It's weird.
Richard	Why are you saying things like that, what do you mean, like …
Louise	Well that's what would be happening.
Richard	She's a woman, you're a woman.
Louise	I don't want to look back and say there were three of us there. I mean I just feel it is such a personal thing and it is something that is potentially so intimate between me and you.
Susie	Right … Richard, is this you again feeling that your mum is sort of a proxy for something you don't know how

to do, whereas actually what Louise wants is for you to be there with her?

I can understand you are not sure you can do it, but I don't think your mum can do it for her – or for you.

Richard   I'll be there, I'll be there. I'll hold her hand, you know I'll like – you know, I'll say the things that I need to say.

Louise   Yep but see you get – look at your body language, you're funny about it.

Richard   What is this?

Louise   Well you can't even look at me, you've leant forward, you are looking at me like over your shoulder, like I'm an imposter.

I am your partner, we made a baby.

Richard   Yeah, yeah, alright, alright.

Louise   I want you to stop putting things in the way between me and you. Not your mum, not your business, not your time away, not your cheque book. I just want it to be me and you.

Where have you gone? That's what I want to know.

Richard   Yeah, alright, alright, you're right.

I was wishing that I could shush Louise again so that Richard's words could be heard by both of them and they could clear some ground but now it is Louise's turn to go zigzagging off ... her statement is strong but timing is all and I wished I could slow it.

13

Louise   Well we've come here for therapy and that's really good,

Richard   I'm just not, I'm just …

Louise   He's paying for the therapy and that's really good.

Richard   You know …

Louise   I see the effort but where are you?

Richard   That's why we're here right, that's why we're here, because I've made the effort and put the, you know, the things in place that we can come here, so that we can share what's going on.

Louise   But paying for them is not a substitute for intimacy, it's not.

Richard   You talk about money because you know it is always going to be there in some way because I am always going to be providing it, so that is why you have got such a whimsical view on money.

And we are off again … This time it's Richard who can't hear what Louise has said about money being a poor substitute for intimacy.

Louise   Don't talk to me about being whimsical about money.

Susie   OK, so here's what I think, when you get to the thing that needs to be said, one of you goes off. So you were saying something, Louise, about how you want Richard to be there, or pointing out he

14

wasn't. He was saying yes, OK. And maybe that yes, OK – his acknowledgement – is the thing that you need to hear, rather than the two of you escalating it.

I think it is a scary moment for both of you, and a precious moment for both of you, or a precious time, and I think a little bit more tenderness rather than leaping on each other with how you are disappointing each other is required, because I sense you are both very disappointed in each other.

Richard Yeah … look I am going to be more engaged, I am going to be more present, I just need you to be able to see that sometimes I'm blocked.

Susie Uh-huh.

Louise Do you want this baby?

I'm not surprised she says this rather aggressively because Richard has gone into a yes-mode, which is actually dismissive, rather than a being-there mode. He's leaned back again into the corner of the sofa. His words seem pro-forma. I sense he is not purposefully dismissive but rather feels out of his depth.

Richard Yeah, yeah, of course I want the baby.

Susie What was that actually? Were you trying to say, Louise, I have missed you or I am insecure, or …

Louise I do feel disappointed and I just feel really upset all the time … and I feel rejected before it has even

begun, I feel it is pushing us apart. The more my
belly grows it is like a wall pushing in the way.

I think there is something about her saying a wall pushing
in the way that allows Richard to go into a reverie and share
what's been troubling him.

Richard   You know, I don't know, it's funny, like the other
day I was looking through my, you know, just some
papers, and I don't know, I come across my birth
certificate and it was weird moment because you
know, it had my mum's name on it but it didn't have
my dad's name on it. Where it said Dad it was just
two dashes, you know, and I just thought that was
weird, it was kind of, I don't know, it felt like it was a
sign.

Louise   A sign of what?

Richard   I don't know, I don't know what, I just felt like it was
saying something to me, do you know what I mean?

Susie   That there is a void?

Richard   Yeah.

Susie   Where your dad was?

Richard   Yeah.

Susie   And so you are not sure what you have got to bring
to your baby and to Louise, and so you go and work
like a madman?

Richard   Yeah.

Susie   As a way to do something?

I'm thinking now of how Richard's concerns – albeit largely unconscious up until now – about how present and adequate he can be, have turned into being a provider and working for the soon-to-arrive family. He feels himself to be active in response to the forthcoming arrival so he feels rather put upon by Louise and her definition that she is doing everything.

Richard   Yeah, I guess.

Susie   Um, um.

Louise   Baby, you're going to be an amazing dad, you are just going to be amazing, you are. You are nothing like that thing, that void, that man, you're not.

You don't have to be anyway.

Like that's why we were always going to have kids, it was always going to happen, and you were always going to be brilliant.

So Louise now has turned her panic and accusation into idealisation, and it is true that Richard is in a different place because he has had a chance to say why he is so frightened. We are ending the session with a sense of two different emotional states going on, two different emotional journeys, extreme intensity and preoccupation on both their parts and the possibility that they might understand what the other is feeling.

What's important for the therapist to convey is that being on the same page with the baby doesn't mean having the same emotional response to this event. Louise isn't going to feel as Richard does. Richard isn't going to feel as Louise does. Being on the same page means having an ear out for how the other is feeling and respecting where each other is coming from. In the best of all possible worlds we might be gently suggesting to each member of the couple to become curious about the why of their partners' feelings.

Susie   Alright so …

Louise   Yeah.

Susie   See you next week.

Louise   OK.

Richard   Yeah, thank you.

Susie   Unless of course …

Louise   The baby comes.

Richard   Unless of course.

Louise   *Laughing.* Yeah.

Susie   OK.

Richard   Thank you.

Susie   Alright.

Louise   It's got to wait anyway, we've got to finish decorating the bedroom.

Richard   Yeah I'll get onto that, don't worry about that.

Louise   Thanks Susie, see you next week.

Richard   See you next week, yeah, thank you.

Becoming a parent is momentous. Moving from being a couple to being a parenting couple is challenging. In this session we have been seeing Richard's concerns expressed as flight. Louise's ways of coping are focused on getting everything ready for the baby and in trying to get Richard to behave more like part of a couple. Her anxiety is an equally potent force as is her initial incomprehension about his concerns, but in this session the focus has been on helping Richard to recognise his fear.

Both Richard and Louise bring the imprint of their relationships with their own parents to the pregnancy. Richard's mother has been a very available lone parent who has done everything in the household and looked to Richard to be financially responsible at a young age and to help support her. He has managed that since he left school at seventeen. Louise has become the next woman he is looking after financially.

Louise's mother was quite controlling of her, her sibling and the rest of the family. Her dad was around but disengaged and Louise's mother would mutter about how neglectful or useless he was. Louise hated her mum's way of being and was drawn to Richard because he was much more laid-back and gave her a lot of space, but as she moves into being a mother, the family constellation is stimulated in her. She sees Richard acting like her father and she has become controlling and full of complaints. She doesn't like it – and we've discussed it – but as her isolation grows, it has become almost a default.

In a couple, one sees the trace of the family stories each member emerged from. Often, of course, these are supportive and nourishing. Even so, there may be aspects of their upbringing that they have disliked and have consciously chosen not to reproduce, but when the going gets tough, the difficult bits of the relationships that made them can come to the fore. There is no formula in working with a couple. The endeavour is to give each member the extra beat to hear what the other is saying and wanting while bcoming clear enough to express what's on their own mind. That process can illuminate the unconscious entwinements and longings which need addressing. Each couple's story is different and surprises and touches me in unexpected ways. It is the details that I always find enchanting and affecting. Richard's discovery of the two dashes and Louise's bluntness about not wanting his mum in the delivery room. Such details create an empathic curl and warmth in me as I get to know them better.

Harriet

I've been seeing Harriet for six months. She has recently separated from her long-term partner and has moved out of their shared home.

Harriet came to the UK from Zimbabwe when she was a little girl. She works in a primary school as the school secretary. She comes in bundled up from the cold, a maroon and yellow swirly scarf, nearly as big as her, wrapped around her neck and covering her dark blue coat. She feels very small as she sits forward in the middle of the sofa.

There aren't many words in the session but it feels to me as though we are connected through the active quiet we hold together. We are not at a loss with each other, or separated by the quiet. The quiet is full of feelings which the session explores.

Susie	Hello.
Harriet	I'm a bit slow to get started these days. I'm sorry to have been late.
	God it's cold. I'm just going to be still for a moment, is that OK? …
	Long pause.
	I feel as if I don't know why I am here today.

Susie   *My pause matches hers.* Uh-huh.

Harriet   Well, I feel as if I could have – no, I was thinking about not turning up, but then – oh sod it, yeah, I thought, it's too late to change my mind. I made the commitment… *Wry laugh.*

How was your Christmas?

Susie   Tell me about yours.

Harriet   Quiet, it was quiet.

I didn't want anyone around me, but my sister and my nephew came on Christmas Eve, that was lovely, it was good.

And then, there was a point when I really wanted them to go.

Susie   Uh-huh.

Harriet   Yeah.

Susie   *Long pause.*

Because you needed to return to and be with yourself?

Harriet   Yeah.

Pause.

Susie   Sad … or maybe depleted?

Harriet   Of course.

Everything has changed.

Everything has changed so much in such a short time.

I wanted to be on my own. That was good, that was good. That was right.

I *am* on my own for the first time in such a long time, and the idea of trying to show face, keep up, seem all Christmassy jolly … no. I couldn't. I didn't want to do it.

I did have invites and that was lovely. I was pleased about that …

Sorry – sorry, sorry, sorry.

I don't know what Harriet is saying sorry for but I sense that if I ask I will be interrupting.

Oh, and I hate saying sorry all the time, I hate saying sorry.

Long pause.

How did I get here?

That's what I have been thinking about the last few weeks, Susie. I'm haunted by a sense that one makes a decision and then a path opens up from that decision.

Everything I have been born with, grown up with, aspirations, hopes, oh … it's all gone askew …

It sounds so naff doesn't it, it sounds so naff.

The words aren't conveying the emotional dejection Harriet is transmitting so I try to give her some.

Susie   You are heartbroken, and bewildered, and lost, and it is going to hurt like hell and be incredibly confusing.

Harriet   *Crying with desperation.*

How long is it going to take, how long is it going to take?

Harriet is in shock. She is slowly trying to assimilate a loss, a loss that can't find a place in her mind. A loss that doesn't want to be true. She doesn't know how she got to where she is. She is in a state of grief where it is hard for her to be with people and genuinely present for more than a few minutes.

Harriet needs to be heard, by which I mean she needs her experience validated by herself and by me. She's aching to be understood so that she can understand herself and what has happened. She needs somebody with her who can bear to go into the horror and the bleakness she feels. Her sorrow touches me deeply.

Harriet   I don't understand what I did wrong, I don't understand. Maybe I took too long trying to have a child, maybe I took too long, maybe I enjoyed myself too much.

I am forty-six years old and I don't understand what on earth is going on.

If you had asked me ten years ago, everything was brilliant. I could see, I could see forward, right now everything is just … *Pauses.*

Susie   Well, things are blocked and frozen.

Harriet   I don't understand how to get out of it. I don't like this feeling.

Susie   Tell me, what is this feeling, because when I said blocked and frozen, you put your hand in front of your mouth?

I'm always observing and, at the same time, almost experiencing a modified version of what the person I am working with is conveying. In order to be with Harriet in the pain she finds herself in, I take on, in a minuscule way, for the time we are together, the flavour of her pain. This is a form of empathic identification which inevitably occurs for the therapist.

Being a therapist is a peculiar activity because a part of oneself is highly emotionally open, almost relaxed as one reflects on what is being said and how it is being said and the way in which feelings are expressed. Simultaneously, we are feeling ourselves in our patients' shoes as we dwell with them in their pain and confusions and so, without knowing it, I have noticed Harriet's hand in front of her mouth. A part of me recognises the conflict she's experiencing between wanting to express herself and wanting to stop her words.

My question to her about her hand in front of her mouth is thus not thought out, it is spontaneous and curious.

Her physical presence in the session is characterised by a kind of folding in on herself. She looks quite tiny sitting on the sofa but she isn't a small woman. The image that comes to me is that of a hibernating dormouse: hiding herself away until she can emerge from her frozen winter. When I tell her about her hand gesture, she looks up at me.

Harriet   *A little laugh.* I can see that now you have pointed it out. I am very aware that I do that now, because I feel if I don't hold it back, it is going to be an avalanche.

        It is going to be huge, and I am scared of that.

Harriet fears being overwhelmed. On the one hand she needs stillness, and on the other she needs words around her experience and the devastation she is feeling.

Harriet and her partner had had two rounds of IVF. They were both unsuccessful and she left the home they had lived in together for six years.

Susie   You didn't know that you weren't able to conceive.

Harriet   No.

Susie   In facing that, in coming to terms with that, the theft of a future, the theft of being able to carry a baby.

Harriet   *Sob.* What do I do?

Susie   Well it's a double loss isn't it, Harriet, because you are dealing with the loss of your partner too, so you are very much at sea.

I don't address Harriet's question directly. I know that it is unanswerable. My job is to find a way to help her live through this anguish.

People wonder how something unbearable and unanswerable moves to become accepted, albeit a bumpy accepted.

What therapists observe in their practice is that the more space there is for the expression of the complex feelings that such an event throws up, the more the capacity for mourning and loss can occur.

Loss is not a full stop. It is important to recognise and experience because in time the loss itself can move from being a present terror to a sadness that can be lived with. Outside of the therapy room, people may wish to jolly Harriet along, or avoid her pain or be extra careful not to bring up the loss she has experienced. This is all done out of compassion and caring but it hasn't and doesn't help Harriet.

Harriet   But I am not the only one, I know it happens to so many people, I know that, and I wasn't stupid going into it, the treatment, I wasn't stupid, but God I was hopeful.

Susie   Ah ... ah.

Harriet   So I am finding it very hard to look at you today.

Susie   Uh-huh.

Harriet   How do you think I am doing in terms of managing all of this? It's not strange, is it?

Susie   I think it is very strange for you to find yourself in this situation and very painful, and also I don't know if there is some sense of shame that you are carrying.

Harriet   … yes, I do feel terrible shame …

It is almost like I was smelling shame. People communicate the subtlety of their feelings and therapists are trained to catch them. It was only a whisper but it came through to me. The clinical situation with its frame by frame speed slows down and reveals what otherwise can go unheard, unseen or unfelt. And so it was with Harriet's shame.

I think about her shame as being injurious to her sense of self. It is as though the shame comes in to protect her from the hurt that is in every one of her pores.

When you are drenched in shame, it stops other kinds of thinking and feeling. You are in a closed loop where it is hard to release the sorrow. But what will allow Harriet to live with meaning beyond this loss will be an ability to experience and then digest her pain, not be defended against it by shame.

Feelings are central to the work of psychological change. Feelings seem so ordinary and yet they can give us the biggest problems if we can't engage with them. When we misperceive what we feel, for example, show anger, which can easily be stimulated and which doesn't seem to dissipate, then we might ask, is anger a 'cover' feeling; a feeling that the individual is accustomed to experiencing, ever available to be stirred up and yet, once felt, fails to relieve the individual. If we probe, we may be able to enable a wider spectrum of feelings, such as disappointment, hurt, loneliness, fragility. Such feelings, once experienced, may move the individual who is 'stuck'. Enabling and receiving the complexity of feelings and tuning into them accurately allows them to change as much as interpreting unconscious ideas.

Susie   It was a sense I felt when you said you couldn't look at me, and I was trying to understand the difficulty of you seeing me see your pain.

The tough thing is you just didn't get pregnant, and *that* you are not responsible for.

It is just absolutely awful, and I think it can be quite difficult to hold onto that awfulness and so you might go into shame, or it's my fault, when it just is.

Harriet   *Crying.* It *is* my fault, I am forty-six years old and I don't know whether I can afford to pay you next time and I can't – I don't know where I am going to be living in the next week – I don't understand; how did I get here?

And I don't want to be a victim, I don't feel as if …

Susie   OK, so you are in a really bad spot. You chose to leave. You did it in a way …

Harriet's shame has closed her thinking down. She's shamed by the idea of being a victim, of being poor, of being in an unstable housing situation. She's alone. She's isolating herself and she's stuck.

Harriet   I couldn't stay.

Susie   OK, you couldn't stay, but actually that was also your home.

Harriet Oh, it was too sad, it was too sad, it was too sad. I couldn't bear myself around him. He never got angry, he never got angry. Waiting to see his sadness was so overwhelming. His sadness was so overwhelming.

I am thinking about how his pain was unbearable for Harriet because it also augmented her own pain, but knowing some of her background I am also thinking of a curious parallel experience which she has enacted from her earlier life.

She left her partner after six years, following the failure of the second round of IVF. This mirrors an earlier departure when she came to England from Southern Africa with her mother at the age of six. Her father stayed behind. This leads me to reflect on departures, and the suddenness of a rupture, and the impossibility for her of feeling she has the power to remake her relationship. She has exiled herself from her flat, from her partner with whom she suffered the loss of the promise of a baby and hence the future they had envisioned.

Harriet This feels like an indulgence.

Susie   Um, um, but you know what comes across as so poignant is the two of you sobbing inside in your deep anguish but not able to speak.

When your dream collapsed, you both went into a silo, or you went into a silo. The hurt caused you shame and that makes sense of why you can't really be around people for very much time now.

I'm trying to get a counter rhythm into the flow between us. Not to stop Harriet's horror but to play another tune alongside it. A tune that interrupts the doomed, inevitable, closed-down quality of the decision she made to leave her flat and partner.

Harriet   Yeah.

Susie   And I wonder whether you also feel an embarrassment that you don't think you can pay to come.

Harriet   That's my point. I need to come but I have so little.

Susie   That you feel that you don't have things to give.

Harriet   I don't. I feel awful about that … I can't believe right now … I don't know how I am going to balance things in the next month, that's the reason I didn't think I was going to come today, but then I went well, you've booked in, you have to pay, if you don't go you still have to pay.

Susie   You made a certain set of choices in extremis, didn't you, and now you are thinking about those and their impact on you.

Harriet   Yeah.

Susie   And one of those is financial. It's not the only thing, but I think maybe it *is* time to reconsider. That's what you say: *How did I get there, how did I do this,*

> *how did this happen?* That's what we are looking at,
> and I think we will have to just put the finance bit
> between us on the side for the moment.

Harriet I don't want to be owing, I don't want to be
beholden.

Susie No, I wouldn't do it that way. I don't think that would
work. We need to agree that there is an amount
that you could manage, and that is what you will
pay because I also don't want you to be in an owing
situation, I don't think that would be right.

Harriet *Whisper.* Thank you, thank you.

Susie Will you think about what is plausible, honestly.

Harriet Honestly I will.

Susie And I will see you next Tuesday.

Harriet OK.

I am thinking about how things that are incomprehensible
can make an individual feel quite helpless and the psyche
doesn't like feeling helpless. We would rather make ourselves
responsible, we would rather change everything around to
make ourselves the centre of our own misfortune. That then
becomes a way of understanding. It also is the magical lever
used in everyday thought, *if only I'd never started, I wouldn't be...
if only I'd studied I could have got an A ...*

We can either find that we blame ourselves or we can blame

others and see things as their fault. Both those propositions keep people stuck.

Therapy can sidestep these two positions. It's a place to explore all the losses, the things gone wrong, the long held anguishes, but it is not a place just to hide. It is a place to lift off the blame to see how Harriet has handled what has occurred. It is a place for her to think and feel whether she has more options than the shamed, sorry-ness.

In time it will be a place for her to re-engage with her relationship with her boyfriend and to see whether she and he want to remake it. To see, too, whether the abruptness of the departure which was driven by the horror of the pain she felt herself and saw in her partner, can be managed differently. And to consider whether her leaving was a kind of imprint from her childhood separation; a behaviour which she can now give up.

The sadness may not disappear, but it is something they both experienced and perhaps can support each other through. They wanted to make a family together. That desire was an expression of their love. Remaking that love in the face of their shared and separate loss could be a part of a deep, renewed, coming together again.

Harriet's departure from Zimbabwe was not something she could understand. She was a little girl who obviously wasn't in control of it and not much was explained to her. She lost the smell of her early childhood. She lost the scenery of her childhood. She lost the customs of the town she came from. She lost her extended family. She lost contact with her father too. I'm aware of the way she phrases things: *How did I get here?*

And that's what I have been thinking about the last few weeks, that sense that one makes a decision and then a path opens up from that decision. She also says *I don't understand what I did wrong, I don't understand.* These words strike me as the sense of bewilderment that accompanied part of her childhood: *How did I get here? I don't understand what I did wrong, I don't understand.* They are a refrain of incomprehension, of what could not and cannot be explained.

Harriet's sense of helplessness is an example of a phenomenon we humans struggle with. We don't like to be helpless. And yet her sense of being helpless is real and psychically accurate. It throws her back to an early helplessness, also real but unexplained. To a six-year-old, that must have seemed inexplicable. So her feeling of helplessness is not a neurotic feeling to run away from. It is a difficult feeling to accept. But acceptance is what will in time help.

Much of the time we want to order and classify our world. We plan and strategise. We analyse and we count. We find comfort in binaries such as good or bad, excluded or included, friend or foe, right or wrong. Cultures vary in what is designated in the binary but the existence of these classifications, this splitting of experience into black and white is ubiquitous. Harriet is feeling the intensity of the sad feelings. That makes absolute sense. So do the feelings of helplessness which we, as a culture, have difficulty accepting.

I am raising issues of categorisation and complexity not in relation to her feelings but in relation to her defenses shielding other feelings. Defenses try to protect one but in doing so they throw up other feelings which are powerful deterrents against engaging with more fundamental feelings, in her case tolerating her sense of helplessness.

From the psychoanalyst's perspective the splitting categorising mechanism can also be thought of as developmental. Developing minds feel safer with bad things stored outside of themselves – projected on to malevolent characters such as those we encounter in fairy tales. And as children order their world, the allowed, not allowed, and the attribution of difference forms a mental picture of how the world is. It is a way of ordering the world and a way of trying to control it.

Gradually, the child begins to recognise that other minds exist and they think and feel differently – not worse than, not better than, just differently. This development is both troublesome and exciting to the child as she or he begins to navigate opinions and desires that are personal and idiosyncratic. If all goes well, the child's expression of her or his opinions and desires will be welcomed and a confidence will emerge that underpins the sense of being both attached to others while having a sense of one's own being.

This separated-attachment idea depends upon being sufficiently securely attached in the first instance. If that has not occurred, if those who raise us have not had us in mind as a separate person who is simultaneously vulnerable and dependent, then the sense of self that develops may feel insecure. A search for certainties will ensue as well as a form of thinking that is caught up in good and bad, in and out, them and us and so on until new relationships in therapy, friendship or love relationships provide for what attachment researchers and therapists called 'earned security'.

Psychoanalysis and psychological theories of development see the capacity to hold complexity in mind – which is to say when thinking is not arranged in banishing binaries – as a hallmark of psychological selfhood.

This is not to say that right and wrong are not useful categories but they are not uniformly useful categories. They pertain to certain situations, ethics, morality and so on, but in the realms of emotions, and often in politics, over-simplification is a detriment. It diminishes our capacity to hear another. It dilutes the richness of our inner life and opinions. It weakens our resilience and it flattens public discourse.

Complexity is essential to thought. There is rarely one story, one subjectivity, one way to look at and evaluate things.

A psychoanalyst is always thinking about the backstory of the person sitting with them. So before we leave Harriet I would be asking myself: What were the family in Zimbabwe responding to when they made the decision for Harriet, her siblings and her mother to leave? What were the political, social and psychological conditions which came to make that decision? Beyond that, how did the consequences of emigration and immigration and the loss of family play psychologically for Harriet's mother and father and grandparents? How did Harriet's mother cope with her disrupted life and what did she convey to Harriet about loss? Was it unspeakable, disastrous? How did her mother deal with being transplanted to a new country? Did Harriet experience her first double loss when she arrived in the UK bereft of her father and wider family and with a mother who too would have been bewildered and possible preoccupied as she made a new life. And, how did the smaller family unit find pleasures and were they acknowledged?

I'm spelling this out because complexity and category making are the dialectical prerequisites of being human. We all struggle with the tension between the two poles of questioning and certainty. Out of that tension comes enormous creativity.

Jo

Jo is in her thirties. It is her first session. She bounces in, lively and nervy. She sent me an email requesting therapy saying only that she'd gone off track. She acts with an unusual mixture of nonchalance and diffidence as she enters the room. She has a London accent, and an expressive face, which is engaging. She speaks at a great pace.

Jo   Hi.

Susie   Hello, I'm Susie.

Jo   I'm Jo. Am I really late? I am so sorry, it's just that I think you gave me the wrong address and I don't normally get stuff like that wrong, which is why I'm late and I think I have now wasted like fifteen minutes or something.

Susie   Come in, just go straight ahead.

I'm really sorry, it would be a bit unusual.

Jo   Is it in here?

Susie   Yes, would you like to take a seat on the sofa?

Jo   Yeah, oh god I did not want to start it like this. I didn't want to come in as a wreck.

It's just one of those days where everything goes wrong.

43

Susie   Um, um.

Jo   Anyway.

When I meet someone for the first time, I am really interested to hear what they have to say and how they say it. I notice the pauses, the way their voice gets louder or softer. I notice their physical being and I notice their impact on me. We learn a surprising amount in a first encounter about the themes an individual is struggling with and how their mind has construed their situation in such a way that they can't find exit points from their difficulties. As we listen, we are assessing whether we believe we will be able to be of use to them. Therapy is not for everyone. Sometimes just a single session will be helpful.

What is said in a first session does not become stuck in stone. The content will shift or something unbidden may emerge in session twenty. But how the individual frames her or his dilemmas will be the opening guide.

Jo is late and she says she has been given the wrong address. I know something has gone awry here because she received my correct address on email. So I am alert to what those two things might tell us about Jo's way of being in the world and being with herself. Jo comes in a bit flustered, breathy and busy, and my ears are open to hear how she gets in the way of herself.

Susie   So, tell me.

Jo   Yeah, yeah, I guess I am here because I am unhappy. I'm an actress, well – god, I say I'm an actress, I'm not an actress because I work in a café, I *was* an actress. I was a successful actress at a certain level but I haven't had any work for ages. Anyway, my drama school is having the big ten-year reunion.

Susie   Uh-huh.

Jo   Tonight.

But the thing is, it is happening in the club where I work and I have to work because I need the money and they are short-staffed, and I have obviously known about it for a few weeks and I can just feel it getting worse and worse as it gets nearer and nearer, and now it's today.

Susie   Uh-huh.

Jo   And I am not in any position that I thought I would be. And an ex-boyfriend of mine – he, really, if I am honest, really was the only person who actually understood me – he is going to be there and I haven't seen him for ten years.

I haven't really had anything that even comes close to that, you know, because I am the one that finished it, everything is drained from me. I don't know, I don't even know why I am here because the fact is I feel ridiculous now sat here, having just got upset about an ex-boyfriend, ahh, I feel slightly uncomfortable.

Susie   Uh-huh.

Jo   If I'm honest, right now, because I don't …

             Oh I feel ridiculous.

Susie   Well, it can feel a bit ridiculous because you are talking to a complete stranger and trying to give me a picture of the things that concern you.

Jo   Yeah.

I am listening to Jo and I am torn as to what to say to her. I register her panic.

Her words tumble out and tracking what's particularly important for her – whether it's the ex-boyfriend, or the disappointment in her acting career, or some quite other focus – is going to take a while. Her voice is like a screech and then she halts.

I am interested in why she was unable to swap her shift, which is a very ordinary thing to do when you are feeling under pressure. But she wasn't able to think that or make the change and so I am wondering if she is revealing something about the way she inadvertently traps herself.

I feel the intensity of the clamp around Jo's mind. The trap provokes me to think about whether she lives in a story of no exit, of believing she will be the victim. That she will be abject.

When in doubt, a psychotherapist has to keep their mouth shut. The point of therapy is to see how something unfolds. I need to notice the shifts in the emotional temperature as she recounts her story. I am pulled, just as Jo is, into the tension she feels about swapping the shift or rather her not being able to; seeing her classmates and not feeling successful; and seeing the ex-boyfriend; and so I need to wait, to hold onto all of these themes so that I can be of use to her.

Jo   And I don't want people's pity at this reunion tonight which I know they are going to feel because I see it all the time in people's faces, you can see it.

Susie   You see pity or you see compassion?

             You interpret it as pity, is it pity?

Jo   Maybe, yeah, I don't – maybe I'm projecting that onto them, I don't know. *Sigh.*

I am nudging Jo a little bit here to see whether she has any emotional bandwidth.

Jo has used the word projection which is quite useful. It gives me a sense that she might understand that what she thinks and imagines isn't always the case and that she may misinterpret what other people are feeling because of her own difficult feelings about her work life. Her disposition is cheery, high-strung and anxious all at the same time. I feel her slipping between various emotional states within a millisecond. This presumably is her style and I need to respect it but I also want to find a way to slow her down.

Susie   I suppose the important thing for us is to figure out how *you* feel about this.

Jo   I am scared where I will end up.

> I know I keep thinking about the morning that we broke up. We just parted and it wasn't horrible, it wasn't in any way – nobody did anything actually wrong.

Susie   Uh-huh.

Jo   And I just let it go. I can remember it so clearly. I watched him walk, walk away, and actually if I am honest he is the only person that I shared true intimacy with, and I don't know why I gave up on it so easily.

Jo has slowed down and moved into a reflective space. She's now looking at me intently. The pace of her words has changed and I'm feeling that I might be able to be of some help. My question which follows may seem rather hackneyed as it diverts her attention to her earlier life. It comes out of the full stop she seems to have arrived at. I could have waited and not said anything but I was mindful that we only had a very short session and I needed to see what to recommend. She has had the thought that she gave up on the relationship, on him, so easily, many times and is as perplexed now as she was ten years ago.

Susie   And when you think of loss, did you have earlier losses in your life?

Jo   Not really, I don't think so, not that I can …

We are back at another full stop.

Susie	Tell me a bit about your background.
Jo	Well, I don't really know my dad. I didn't know him.
Susie	Is that your phone?
Jo	Oh god, sorry.
Susie	Would you mind turning it off, thank you.
Jo	Hold on a second, oh, I've just got to answer this quickly, I'm really sorry.
	Hello … I um, I'm just at a meeting actually … OK, OK, I'll be there in ten, I'm really sorry, I'm just around the corner.
	Is it OK if I keep my phone on?
Susie	No, I'm afraid it isn't, because I can't really concentrate and we've got such a very short time together and I would really like …
Jo	I'm sorry.

The moment was lost with her and we are sent in a different direction, one that might be very helpful to us to understand as the therapy continues.

We have just talked about the humiliation of the reunion, the loss of the boyfriend and the fact that she didn't know her dad, and I am linking those things in my mind as a possibility. But, before I can think about those connections and whether they are relevant, and certainly before she can feel anything about them, we are off on a train in a completely different direction.

Jo   I'm sorry because now I have completely forgotten what we were talking about.

Susie   Uh.

Jo   I'm not very good at this sort of thing. Is there a right way to do it?

Susie   No.

Jo   OK.

Susie   We just have to get to know each other.

Jo   OK, yup …

Susie   Something led you to be in touch.

Jo   Yeah, my friend who comes to you suggested it might be a good idea, I think. I think actually he was just bored of listening to me going on about how awful my life is, so he just suggested that I come in and pay somebody else to listen to me talk.

Sorry, I am just talking too much, actually I guess that's the point isn't it, but yeah.

Susie   If I'm seeing your friend, I wouldn't be able to see you.

I am nonplussed about this information as I usually know how an individual has come to me and I fear I was a little harsh in rushing to say that I wouldn't be able to see her. I wouldn't, but I wish I could have said it more gently. If I examine myself as to why I was so hasty, I think it is probably because the session has been quite challenging so far, with us having so little time and the disruption of the phone. I was too hurried to manage this third piece of awkward information better.

Jo   Oh.

Susie   But I would be able to think about who might be right and recommend them to you.

Jo   Oh, OK. But the thing is I haven't even – *sigh* – I haven't even told you his name.

            I feel like maybe – I feel like, I feel like you just don't want to see me. I know I've just wasted however much money coming here and it kind of feels like you are dumping me! Like I've just, I've just told you what I have got to go and do tonight, why would you choose to say something like that?

Susie   It's really unfortunate that I didn't know. You knew, of course, but you didn't know that it would preclude me seeing you.

Jo   Well shall we just call it a day then?

Susie   No, sit please.

Jo   I mean there's no point going on, is there really.

Susie   Jo, please sit down because it's not – there's things that we are in the middle of that I think it is quite worth us trying to just hold on to.

Jo   This is just so typical.

            This is really typical of my life because I can't …

Susie   OK, so that's what's very useful for us, isn't it. If it's typical that something doesn't go as you wish, right away you have been bold enough to show me what doesn't work. And I would like to think about who would be the right therapist for you.

Jo   But why wouldn't you be the right therapist?

Susie   I might be the right therapist. Of course I might be the right therapist, I might be very interested to be …

Jo   It just feels like you're fobbing me off to somebody else.

Susie   Um, um.

Jo   Which I wasn't expecting. I just wasn't expecting this.

Susie   No, I can see that, I can see that that's – it's definitely not what you would have wished, but I think maybe in your jumping to the idea of why I'm doing it, and discounting what I am actually saying by making up a different story to yourself, it is inadvertently hurting you, because actually – this isn't about you, it is really about me, it's about me, it's about how I work and the kind of rules or ethics that govern my job.

Even though the impact is hurtful for you, it's not about who you are and how it pleases or displeases me.

Jo is, quite understandably, projecting on to me, a rejection. This echoes the earlier moment when she imagines her class-mates pitying her. It is important to give her the reality here so that she can take back the worry that it is all about how pitiful she is.

It's very interesting when the problem the individual has in part talked about comes alive in a therapy session. Jo's talking about rejection and I find myself bounced into rejecting her. I feel this acutely. Worse, I can't even repair it for her properly and so I have caused her hurt and added to her chaos.

I don't want to have an abrupt ending with Jo: she's had an abrupt ending with the boyfriend from ten years ago and I am imagining that her father disappeared when she was very little, although I don't have any confirmation of this. I do know that I can't be of use to her if I am seeing her friend. Hearing about her through someone else's eyes, or seeing her friend through her eyes, isn't really the point. Therapy is a sealed environment. We aim to hear things first-hand and then assess them with the person concerned. We look for the discordances rather than hearing them elsewhere. It's not perfect because people are not always reliable reporters of their own behaviour, but we do need to see things from their perspective as we add in ours. Knowing something from someone else does influence one and although that can be useful, it can also be distorting.

Such rules were hard learned through years of experience in the psychoanalytic journey. Initially, Freud and his followers saw people who were friends and colleagues and holidayed with some of them, but as psychoanalysis became a mainstream practice in the United States after the Second World War there was enough accumulated experience to see that friendships weren't the wisest of structures for a practice. It made it all a bit too cosy and sometimes rather muddled.

It's not practical in today's world to know nothing of one's patients except what they show and tell. The internet has put paid to that. Then too, they have information about their chosen practitioner, indeed they may well have researched you before they approach you. They can know a great deal more about the therapist than what the therapist shows of her- or himself through their demeanour in the consulting room.

A therapist might be asked, for example, how her daughter enjoys such and such a college, the patient having discovered through a couple of clicks what university the therapist's daughter has attended. When such information is brought to the therapy it can have a significance beyond the simple enquiry. The therapist might be interested in why this particular patient has asked this of her and as she enquires about it, the patient might be flummoxed. The question was for her part innocent.

When I say it has a significance, I am not implying that this is misbehaviour or inappropriate on the analysand's part, I'm signalling rather that it can become an additional form of communication in the therapy relationship. A query about a daughter's college could mean any number of things, from the patient's straightforward interest to anxiety, to a wish to see the therapist's private life as a guide for her- or himself, to a need to show that her or his daughter is 'doing well', and everything in between. It can sound precious to say we are interested in exploring such questions for what they yield about the patient's inner world but if used judiciously such an interchange can be productive.

But back to Jo, for whom such questions are hardly on the table. She got in touch without knowing that my seeing her friend would preclude my taking her on for therapy. She knew my name from him and, as it turned out, had found my details though the internet. For her this was an act of responsibility. She looked me up and found out how to contact me. She didn't know what my rules were. My intention now is to find a way of moving her to somebody else if she decides to pursue therapy. I hope she will be able to do this and that our encounter won't sit as another cut-off where she falls through the cracks.

Jo　　So, well, what do we do now?

Susie　　Well, I think what I'd like to do is see you again for a full session and see whether you actually want to pursue therapy, and for me to see who comes up in my own mind that I think would be good for you.

Jo　　Yeah, I'm not sure that I do want to pursue therapy.

Susie　　That's understandable … but perhaps the idea will sit with you.

Jo　　I guess I need to think about it. I don't want to make any big decisions because that's what's gotten me in trouble. Thank you.

Susie　　OK.

Jo　　And I'll be in touch.

Susie   OK.

Jo   Alright, thanks.

Jo's had a difficult first session and she has a tricky night to navigate. Despite our difficult meeting, I hope that she will be back for a proper assessment and referral.

A therapist, of no matter how much experience, cannot predict how the words that are said in a session will settle in. It is one of the peculiarities of the analytic encounter: the psychotherapist puts her- or himself out to try understand the dilemmas the other is grappling with but we can't know which words – certainly not in early sessions – will resonate. Individuals and couples come to their ensuing sessions having found something illuminating that the therapist may not have noticed had much salience. We can't always calibrate things. The therapist is always increasing, and revising, her or his knowledge and understandings of the person and they way they receive the words shared in the session.

This is not to say that a therapist doesn't know what she is doing. Of course not. It is to say that the human psyche is intricate, surprising, and that while consciously things may make sense, the more unconscious processes are also in train and do not reveal themselves in a logical sequence.

Helen

Helen is in her late twenties. She has been coming to see me for eighteen months. She's very much a privileged middle-class Londoner, hyper-cosmopolitan, well-travelled and, along with her contemporaries, sees herself working in New York, Hong Kong or Sydney for a time. She was very successful at school and university and has landed a job in a prestigious law firm. She's tall, with blonde hair, long fingers and an inviting smile. Outwardly, she's extremely confident but inside, troublingly insecure. She's planning to marry Rob, her boyfriend of three years. He's a heart surgeon, warm and supportive and comes from a similar background. Of late she has been interested in discovering a bit more about her inner life and what makes her tick but she's skittish and sticking with an idea or feeling isn't easy.

Helen   How are you?

Susie   OK thanks.

Helen   I had a bit of an, um, just a bit of a weird weekend really.

I just did, um, something just, ah yeah …

Um, I was at this thing and I ended up ahh, um, I don't really know how to, sorry, I'm …

Long pause.

Helen is in danger of stalling and I sense she needs a question to get some words out.

Susie   Where were you? What was it?

Helen   It was just a work thing but I just … Oh …

I just, like, slept with this man.

Susie   Uh-huh.

Helen   Emotionally and morally it's not OK, but physically it's just someone's skin on your skin, you know.

Susie   Who was this guy?

Helen   He is just a partner in a different firm that I know – it just, this thing, he just was sort of looking at me and …

And he was saying some stuff and I just did it … I just did it. In a moment I just did it. I don't know why … I don't really know.

I'm aware of pace here. Helen is taking a while to tell me what she wants to say but as soon as she has, she is almost racing along describing to herself what she's done.

Susie   Would you want to discover why?

Helen   Yeah, I guess, but …

Susie   How old?

Helen   I guess fifties.

Susie   Uh-huh.

Helen   It makes me feel very sick thinking about the actual
bit, 'it', but I think weirder because of Rob. It is just
not like me, I don't do that kind of thing, you know,
like I just, I have never done that, and yeah I am just
not that kind of person really.

I'm really interested in Helen's use of language. She says this
thing, it, I don't really do this kind of thing. I am holding this
speech pattern in a bubble to try to understand what it is that
has happened in this encounter.

Susie   So you have surprised yourself.

Helen   Yeah.

Susie   In an uncomfortable way.

Helen   Yeah.

Susie   And were you uncomfortable with Rob last night?

Helen   Yeah in my head, yeah, but not outwardly.

Susie   Yes, we know that is your tendency, isn't it. You are
incredibly skilled at being …

Helen   I know.

Susie   Apparently available to everybody or …

Helen   I know, I know.

Susie   Thinking things – conveying that things are just fine.

Helen   Umm.

Susie   When you actually have things inside of you that are disturbing and now it's …

Helen   *Crying.* Sorry …

Crying … *Long pause.*

Susie   What's going through my mind …

Helen   Yeah.

Susie   Is that you have been trying to bring more of yourself to yourself.

When I say she is trying to bring more of herself to herself, I'm referring to those cut-off parts of Helen that she doesn't really know much about. Her psychological energy was harnessed to achieve from early on. She went to a London girl's private school, and after a gap year travelling through Thailand, Australia and New Zealand, she read Law at Cambridge. She was then recruited to a Golden Circle law firm. The backstory is that Helen's mother was well off and middle class. She did not develop a career outside the family. She was stopped from doing so by her own mother's disapproval and a lack of encouragement from her husband.

Helen is the eldest of four and was designated to carry her mother's unfulfilled ambition. In doing so, and doing so well, she didn't discover her own desires or her own ambition. She's arrived where she's meant to be but there's an emptiness and a sense of purposelessness. The attributes she has developed don't feel integral to her; more as though they are stick-ons.

In the therapy we are tentatively addressing the rather undeveloped aspects of her.

Helen   Yeah but I don't know who that is. I don't know that I know who I am.

There's a plea in her voice, a hopeless cry almost of not knowing the territory of who she is. It's not anything as crude as being a good girl, although there is that, but it is a sense of being opaque to herself. I feel her frustration. She wants to feel more alive but a low-level depressive state lies behind her charm and what's depressed is this undeveloped and unknown part of her.

Susie   I know, and so maybe this is what this episode is about. It's a blip. It stands in contrast to your competence in everything and being perfect and just lovely to Rob which may have precluded discovering other things. Blips aren't just smudges that need to be rubbed out. They can be useful to you.

You are considering marrying him, maybe you want to show him a bit of your confusions and your …

Helen   I just – just the thought of like expressing that to him is just really – I don't know, just the idea of actually having like, I don't know, talking about this stuff.

Susie   A conversation?

Helen   Um, um. It would just be weird. *Laugh.* A conversation, yep.

Susie	One that starts: oh I don't feel so good, I'm a bit confused.
Helen	I know, but he would just say, why? I don't think he would understand.
Susie	So then you might find the words to answer his why just as you have found them here.
Helen	What? I feel weird that I have slept with this man.
Susie	I don't think that's the issue is it? The issue is …
Helen	Well it feels …
Susie	… that this has cracked something for you, something that you've shown me but you haven't ever taken to Rob. It's the carapace you have which has served you pretty well but it is also …
Helen	It is just like he's really nice, there's nothing …
Susie	Yeah, but it's deprived you. You've felt 'I can't really show who I am, the other aspects'.
Helen	Which ones?
Susie	The muddled bits, the not-so-sure, the one who isn't always striving.
Helen	Yeah, I sort of feel like, I don't know, like I don't know about those things, I feel sort of more – feel a lot …

Reading the words, it sounds like I'm missing Helen. I'm on one track and she is on another. Helen is very interested in concrete thinking, in truths, in facts, but right now something else needs to emerge for her.

I have the impression that I am crowding her out by trying to extend the conversation while being pushed into very concrete thinking. 'Do I tell, don't I tell, he's nice'.

I would like Helen to be able to catch the stray thoughts, the uncomfortable feelings, the things that don't fit, the texture of life that is banished, is sequestered off, is excluded during the day but which causes her anxiety, or rebounds upon her in the morning as she is getting up to go to work.

Helen   Yeah, I sort of feel like, I feel fine.

       What is that look?

Susie   It was a look with a question mark.

Helen   *Laugh.* I feel fine, I just feel fine.

       Long pause.

Susie   Do you think this has got anything analogous with when you feel you need to cut yourself, to wipe out something that's difficult and that what you are doing here is actually trying to bring it here rather than banish it.

Helen's been periodically cutting her arms. She started during her A levels. It has usually been provoked by a difficult feeling or a feeling which overwhelms her that she doesn't know what to do with. The cutting has historically provided some relief. It allows her to sob and wash away her confusions. A growing discovery for Helen in the therapy is that feelings can trickle in without having to be banished. There isn't just an on or an off tap. Most of the time, as we see, she still likes to square things away and when she can't, she can become distraught.

Helen   I suppose I feel sort of quite like lonely a lot of the time.

Susie   Uh-huh.

Helen   But that doesn't make any sense because I am surrounded by people all the time.

Susie   Well, alone isn't the same as lonely.

She looks at me quizzically.

You could be missing some bits of yourself.

This 'lonely' that Helen is now touching on is a crucial piece of her difficulties. It relates to the focus on achieving. Taking exams, getting into the prestigious school and university and law firm and finding a boyfriend with a similar family background, has driven her. They link her to others but it is a lonely linkage as she is only present as a surface.

Living, knowing herself, is a foreign idea. She's intrigued but a bit bemused by the idea that she is lonely.

Helen   But what bits? What am I lonely for? What am I missing?

Susie   The way you have described it to me it seems like instead of these bits of you being tucked inside of you, they are off somewhere else almost outside of yourself. And when they emerge, they kind of boomerang back on you and you find them disconcerting.

I think what we have been trying to do is help you get to know those aspects, and I suppose the weekend was an explosion of something that seems so alien that is usually kept outside of your awareness.

As long as Helen is surrounded by people and tasks and knows what is expected of her, she can function at a very high level. On her own, she isn't really sure of who she is. She feels empty and lost. For her, it's a blessing that she has to work long hours and go along with the mantra of work hard, play hard.

Helen   Yeah. I sometimes feel though, like what is the actual point, like what is the point?

Susie   Um, um.

Helen   What is it actually for? Like why am I getting that person more money and not this person. What am I doing? Am I going to be there at that same place or some other just the same, doing the same things for my whole life?

Susie   Good questions.

Helen   Well, then what? So I just get like – go and work in a surf shop or something. *Laughing.*

Susie   *Laughing.* Can we slow down because I think this is a really good illustration of your thinking processes, which go something like: if I'm critical or uneasy at my high prestige law firm then there's nothing.

Could I ask you to maybe take a pause and see if there are bits that have meaning for you and bits that are difficult, that might be more nourishing?

Helen   Is that the point?

Helen has got a rather black and white reality, so if she is not the successful lawyer and that doesn't make sense to her any more, then she might as well do something designated by her education and social class as useless – to go and work in a shop, as though there is nothing that has meaning. I am trying to slow her up here, to see if she can conceive of herself as having meaning wherever she might be.

At another level, she is asking about the meaning of life – an existential question we can all find ourselves reflecting on from time to time – but which for her has an urgency given that she has, without realising it, been following the lead of others rather than discovering her own.

Helen   Is that the point?

Susie   Well it isn't the point, there are many points.

Helen   What is *the* point?

I was just sitting on the tube on the way in this morning, I was just like right, so this is it, you know, this is the – I have been on this tube forever and I'm going to stay on this tube forever.

But don't you feel it as well? ... *Pause.*

At all?... *Pause.*

Susie   It is very hard to be missing a lot of yourself and your experience.

Helen   Yeah but that is so abstract isn't it. Like what does that actually mean, that you can say that?

Susie   Well, I think what it means is that when you wake up in the morning and you have all of that anxiety, we could try to slow it down and see what it is there for.

Helen   Right – *visibly relieved, she sits up attentive* – OK, yeah, oh right, so it, it's as if it's trying to tell me something is it?

Susie   Yeah, it's both shielding you, but it's also – it's a signal, it's a 'giving you something'.

Helen   Yeah definitely, definitely.

Susie   So maybe we could just consider it without it driving you to take an action. I think when you feel uneasy, you rocket into action. Action has given you a certain comfort but there isn't always an easy resolution or an emotional solution to what's troubling you. Action makes you feel less feeble because you feel yourself to be doing something – but sometimes we need to put action to one side ...

Helen   Um, um, um, um ...

Susie   To consider privately and slowly what the signal is.

Some space might then open up. And in that space questions like do I want to be a lawyer, do I want to be X, what am I feeling now, might emerge and if you don't shut them right down, by actions or attempted solutions, such reflections might lead you to what you are missing that is producing this sense of loneliness.

Helen　　OK. Yes. Yes. That makes a lot of sense …

I feel less jangled.

Yes … Thank you.

Susie　　See you on Tuesday.

Helen　　OK Susie, thanks.

Helen has never found the I in herself. She has followed the path of doing well and it has left her bereft of herself. Now I am suggesting that her internal furniture can be rearranged and there might be quite a few interesting pieces in there that she might be able to sit on, lie on, or enjoy.

I chose not to take up the issues around sexuality or being desired and desiring that sleeping with this older man might suggest. Nor did I pursue with Helen the meaning of the man's age. It's not that I think these issues are insignificant, but therapy always involves judging what is most salient at a given time. I do know from Helen's history that her father – a man now in his late fifties – was quite remote and, from her perspective, controlling. He was a commercial lawyer and Helen has wondered why she has chosen that same branch of law to practice in. He had admired her diligence and taken pride in her prizes at school but he wasn't much interested in recognising her work ambitions. She has longed for his approval for her work success.

She'd been pleased by attention from senior partners – both male and female at the law firm. When she'd described a male partner's approval she has felt a frisson as though she were entering into forbidden territory. It would be easy to interpret this as essentially sexual. I am not convinced that it is. Nevertheless, it does seem to me to have something transgressive about it. The transgression is to do with where she is daring to situate herself and the possibilities that she has now opened up for herself. This contests the view her father had of her. He saw her as delightful but not serious and certainly not someone who should have serious work ambitions.

While she can do the job that she has easily enough, her being seduced by a 'father figure' at another law firm might be Helen's way of getting some undergirding for her ambition from a man similar in age to her father. Her father may not be prepared or able to give this recognition, so she has unconsciously sought it herself, but in doing so she's felt that she's punished herself because the act of sleeping with this man has compromised her morality.

The reader may be wondering, is this a classical oedipal situation? The daughter sleeps with a proxy father? I don't think that is a particularly useful interpretation. The motivation may well be to find support and approval from an older man at work and to unconsciously 'show' her mother that she can be a professional woman and sexual but I am not sure how such an interpretation at this point would help Helen with her struggle to feel authentic in herself.

*

Helen has similarities with several young women that I have seen in my practice over the last twenty years or so. They share a sense of having fulfilled their dreams by getting good jobs, nice enough housing, boyfriends, looking great, being very social, and living a metropolitan life. The heartbreak for me is that this is a generation of women who have grown up with the promise that while the world is their oyster, they have often not had the emotional support to implement it psychologically. Their teachers and parents have told them they can go far and have held open the doors and applauded them. So what do I mean when I say they haven't had the emotional support? The ability to jump through hoops and overcome obstacles has been expected while conflicts and fears they feel about 'advancing' are not really addressed. As feminism moved out of political discourse, replaced by a bizarre assumption that women (and indeed men) can have it all if they tick the right boxes, the importance of conversations about what it means to be breaking new ground has been replaced by an over-optimistic and individualistically focused 'you can do it' philosophy where success is measured by position, money, advancement, looks, and an externally positive attitude.

Paradoxically, the very processes and conversations that enabled women in the seventies to dare to take up new possibilities, the support from contemporaries and the understanding that such daring was both hard and exhilarating, was either not known about by the next generation of parents or was deemed unnecessary since they themselves hadn't gone through it and the world had appeared to open up.

The bequeathing of ambition – often by mothers like Helen's who had not pursued her own – was loving, but it may have been an ambition which denied the fear or the struggles there might be at a psychological level. Thus the complexity of what the young women were engaging with was often hijacked by them finding the next mountain to climb, rather than acknowledging the difficulties they would or could encounter inside of their heads and hearts. The internal voices or conflicts would be silenced rather than have room to breathe and in time dissipate, and this has added to Helen's plaintiff words *What is the point* and *I suppose I feel lonely quite a lot of the time*. In this sense I feel excited that Helen is asking questions about existence and recognising her inner loneliness. It is a good prognosis for her to put her inner life and her outward achievements together.

D. W. Winnicott, a psychoanalyst and paediatrician, understood very deeply the problem of internal alienation. He called this dilemma the False Self. He saw the True Self as an undeveloped part that had not been nourished into life. He proposed that when the main parent, usually the mother, is unable to see and respond to the desire of the child, the True Self goes underground. Resourcefully, the child then finds those aspects that the mother can respond to. This makes the mother feel good in what she is then able to give and the child feel good that he or she has mother's approval and attention. As this pattern of pleasing continues, the True Self fails to come alive and be real for the individual and they live by the compensations the False Self can garner.

The False Self has many attributes and can serve the person well up to a point. Then a chasm between the search for the next challenge and an active life can open up. Helen got to that point which is why she sought therapy. In her therapy, we have been working to understand the False Self organisation as she tentatively invites the dormant True Self to peek above the parapet so that she can get to know her. In time, the False Self (which is better called an adapted self) will join up with the True Self (which is better called a more authentic Helen). She will be enriched and feel she has herself with herself.

Helen has grown up at a time of enormous social change in Britain. Most of the social democratic values which shaped the world after the Second World War have been slowly dismantled. Consumerism, the notion of the individual as a brand and the prevalence of digital life and social media have changed the terms of growing up, especially for young people who have economic resources. The focus on individualism and making it, doing it, being it, selling it, is new. Life can turn into a performance. This is why I've encountered several young women who come in saying their lives are devoid of meaning and purpose. They say that everything is going well on the surface but they feel lost and empty. They have rituals they subscribe to, either around eating/not eating, going to the gym, socialising lubricated by alcohol and cocaine, which they see as crucial. They are digital natives who live with medium-level anxiety a great deal of the time. If we put together the social changes with the psychological difficulties these intensify, we should take seriously the empty feelings many are expressing as an indicator of social and personal malaise.

John

John's in his sixties, he was a union official on the railways. His second wife left him and he came in despair. I have been seeing him for eighteen months.

He's a warm man with a self-deprecating laugh. At the beginning of therapy, he wore his body heavily. He's no small man but it seems to be all of a part of him now. I always hear him huffing and puffing his way up the long staircase to my consulting room. Despite being breathless he begins to talk before he sits down.

John   Oh, what a lovely day. I felt very happy this morning. The sun – I know it's cold but I love this kind of day. It's crisp, wakes you up.

I'm feeling good actually.

Um, I always find it difficult to start speaking, I know it's the way this works … um, um …

Well you know, when I first came here it wasn't, it wasn't me, it just didn't feel right, you know. But it's really worked for me, talking to you … um …

I've never done this kind of thing before, before I met you, and I've talked about things, really intimate things that I've never said to anybody, not even my ex-wife. So, anyway …

Um, that's why I was happy this morning, because I came out and the sun was out and I thought I really, really love this work that we are doing.

Susie   Uh-huh.

John   And I actually wanted to ask you something because … um … I think it was a documentary about therapists I saw and it said – well you know, I come once a week – well, I mean there's people it said on this film, that go like every day to therapy, which you know, six months ago, a year ago, I would have thought – I mean that's ridiculous, indulgent, you know. But then or rather now I thought, maybe I *would* like to come more often to see you actually, and I don't know how often you see people but – I mean, it's really releasing me, talking to you, being here, and I'd like to come three, four times a week because there is so much, you know, in here – *beats his chest* – that I really want to talk to you about.

I was walking up the hill in the sun and I thought I really want to see Susie, I want to see her more, and talk to her more about all these things, and I'm sixty-six and I felt like a young man coming up that hill.

Susie   Uh-huh.

I don't respond to John's request at this point. I don't explore it further as I sense he will tell me more about this impulse.

Coming twice a week could make sense but I am not sure. The rhythm of a weekly session with time to digest things in between has felt right up until now.

John   And I thought why not, you know. I don't want to waste whatever time I've got left. I want to, I want to *really* push forward now in my life. And so I want to come more often and I want to – would I, could I see you outside of the room?

I mean, I know I'm probably breaking every rule in the book, but there's things I do in the week – I don't have many friends – I'm not lonely, but I don't go out with people very much, and there's things I see, I go on walking trips, sometimes I see a film, and I think the only person I want to share this with me is you.

Susie   Uh-huh.

I didn't see this coming.

Of course it isn't unusual for a person to want to see more of their therapist. It isn't unusual that what happens in the outside world is played with reference to the therapist.

The therapy relationship can be a site of emotional truths and connections that aren't yet transferred to the outside world and so the significance of being understood by the therapist can take on enormous power, and as John says, he wants to share the beauty that he is seeing, the reflections he's having, the experiences he is now bursting with.

John	I know I'm probably not meant to say that and …
Susie	It's helpful when you say what's on your mind.
John	Yeah.
Susie	I think what you are telling me is that it's exciting as well as a relief to feel that you can say what you want to say, and discover what you want to say, and look at things afresh, whether it's in this room or outside.
John	Yeah.
Susie	And you are in a hurry and you want to live.
John	Yeah, yes, because I was just walking around half dead for lots of time, you know, for so many years … and I want to – I am in a hurry, um, and you know you said there's not such a thing as I am not meant to say and things I probably shouldn't say but I've got to say, you know, I think I love you Susie, I do.
Susie	Uh-huh.
John	And I know that's wrong and bad and I know it.
	I just think about you all the time, outside. And I have felt like this about a woman many years ago but not for a long, long time.
	I have thought about and I've thought I'll stop myself saying this because it is stupid, but I do, I do love you.
	I'm in love with you and that's why I want to be here and I want to see you outside the room, I want to

share my life with you and I know, I just have these feelings about you. I love you, it's all I've got.

I was walking up that hill and I thought I've got to tell her, I've got to tell Susie that I am in love with her. So I'm sorry but there it is.

Susie I think that's – look, it's important what you've said. I don't want to just put a dagger through everything you have said, but I think part of why this feels really important and special and why our relationship feels so compelling …

John Yeah?

Susie Is because, because I am in this relationship to you, I am listening, I am hearing, I am thinking. I'm feeling with you the struggles you are going through. And that, John, isn't something we could transfer to outside of this room.

This is a delicate moment. The whole of the session is delicate. John finds himself enamoured of me and I have to find a way to acknowledge his feelings without in anyway humiliating him. A declaration of love can be embarrassing if not reciprocated in ordinary circumstances and these are not ordinary circumstances. It's a cliché to say that patients 'fall in love with their therapists' but like all clichés there is something accurate about the intensity of the relationship and the feelings that can be aroused (on both sides) because of the intimacy and sealed nature of the consulting room.

Therapists, or at least this therapist, always falls for some aspects of the person they are working with. I don't mean this in a sexual manner but in the sense that a deep affection, a desire to understand and reach the other, a wish to connect and to be helpful are powerful dimensions of my experience. In order to work with someone for a considerable amount of time and to weather the difficulties we will encounter along the way as they endeavour to change, and with the challenges they will throw at me, the fact of affection will count for a great deal.

In John's case, I feel a profound respect for him in his struggle. His warmth has touched me as has his desire to repair what's gone so wrong. But love in the way he's talking has never occurred to me with him.

John   But I think it could be with us.

Now we are in classical Freudian analysis territory. Indeed, the development of the talking cure pioneered by Freud and Breuer at the end of the nineteenth century depended upon their being able to understand phenomenon that occur in the therapy, naming it as a feature of the therapeutic relationship and then using it in therapeutic work.

The phenomena they called transference describes the often intense feelings an analysand has towards the therapist, stimulated by the therapeutic setting. These include love and longing but they could also include hate or disregard. Such feelings occur in other quasi-authority relationships too but what is particular to psychoanalysis is its study of the transference and the use that can be made of it.

Transference can be understood as a reflection of what is in the individual's unconscious mind about the nature of the relationship. It is a version of his or her experience about how relationships of closeness, mainly learned in the family, pan out. But it isn't simply that. The power of early experience shapes the individual's expectations about relationships in such a way that this psychological imprint is unknowingly foisted onto new romantic relationships. This means that one may treat a teacher like a father, or a boyfriend as a mother without realising it. In new relationships there is often a psychological tussle inside the individual between seeing the loved person, the other, as she or he actually is, and the inner and often unconscious imprint that is held of how previous important relationships have been experienced and therefore will or should be.

To complicate the matter further, there is often the hope of a new relationship fulfilling and fixing the hurts and disappointments from before while at the same time being itself rewritten as an already known relationship.

If an individual has had hard beginnings, love and attachment will not necessarily be straightforward. It could be expressed as over-evaluating the other and not being able to manage when they turn out to be just a person. When the admired one falls off the white steed they are denigrated but that then becomes speedily forgotten and they are reinstated as the person who can, or could, understand, fix and make magic. The transference then is a projection or a stand-in for earlier significant relationships. The therapist is not seen as their own person, nor as a psychological lifeline, but as one whose affection and acceptance is craved.

Of course, the desire for acceptance may be hidden behind porcupine spikes. It may show itself in a testing way through the analysand being irritating, or dismissive, or contemptuous or through an excited kind of love. The transference that emerges – and it can change during the course of a therapy – becomes one of the dimensions of the therapy which comes into play. The therapist examines and shares this with their analysand in the effort to clarify the unconscious processes and projections which may occur.

For Freud, the study of a love transference was predictable. He anticipated that many of the women he saw would fall for him. His take on this was illuminating. He saw transference love – about which he wrote a very important paper, which has been discussed and written about by psychoanalysts many times – as a way for individuals to avoid the work of the therapy. By 'falling in love' with the therapist, Freud argues, they refused to see the unconscious processes at work in their difficulties. They 'fall' in order to sidestep; to be rescued by a father figure of authority and warmth, rather than to investigate the internalisation of the paternal relationship inside of their psyche, to be the child and not the father's partner.

I don't believe this is what John is doing. I take his 'falling' as an expression of his delight in finding that he can be understood and can be open to the world again. I don't see it as a distraction from the therapy but an indicator, as he says, of becoming alive again. That it has landed on me is surely because we have established an important connection. I'm thrilled by his 'coming alive', I treasure it and it makes the work rewarding. I have every expectation that this desire will be available to him in a relationship that will be possible, down the line.

Susie Do you think it's possible, John, that it is this opening up that you fear losing?

I see what's happening for you, especially these feelings towards me, as what has been provoked by your coming to therapy and that, in time, you will be taking this passion and desire into your daily life outside of the therapy.

I think you are looking at it as though it is to do with me rather than what we are doing together, and how it's …

John Yes?

Susie … allowing you to feel a different kind of confidence or realness or …

John *Crestfallen.* Well, you don't. You don't feel it do you?

Um, I … um … I just thought as I walked up that hill, um … I was thinking about all the things we have talked about, the things that have gone wrong I thought, and I know you, you are saying I am holding you up as a way out of dealing with those things … and I just thought I would say it because I thought it's not just that, it is actually about you, Susie …

um, and I thought I have to say it and I thought I can't bear it if she's – *and now he is crying* – if she says no. The thing is I know it's stupid, but I do love you – *crying* – Sorry.

Susie   I don't think it's about sorry and it's not that I am not affected or moved by what you are saying.

I want to suggest that this is about the loss, not just of Meg actually, but of your first wife and …

John   Yeah but …

Susie   … your anguish about not being able to bring yourself to them because …

John   I did, I tried to, well …

Susie   Yeah, but not just you. *They* couldn't either, it's …

John   But that's why we connect so well, it's like, that's what I didn't have with them.

Susie   Yes, but I'm not a wife.

John   I know but …

Susie   I'm not a partner. I'm a partner in the search to help you … find those aspects of you that haven't been able to be alive for you. And you've become interested in your life so that you've become a curious man. You've got passion, a beating heart and your senses and emotions are opened up.

John   Yeah.

Susie   And I think we have got a lot more time to spend together within this context.

John   But I think about you, like in bed, and I'm sorry, I do, I really want to make love to you.

Susie   Uh-huh.

John   And I …

Susie   But does it make sense if I say, I think that you're wanting to show your gratitude?

I think we can both treasure that and appreciate that you feel very affected by being attached and cared for and thought about here.

John   Yeah.

Susie   And you know how seriously I take your troubles.

John   Yes I do.

Susie   And you know, the ways in which we both enjoy the things that have been changing for you.

John   Yeah.

Susie   But I think that we need to hold this together between us and just …

John   Yeah, um …

Susie   Because it is not going to happen and I want to continue to be available to you.

John   Yeah … yeah … no, I'm sorry.

You're not going to kick me out or turn me away because this means so much to me, being here?

Oh dear, I feel terrible now. *Laugh*.

Susie	Can we go at it the other way around? Can I say that it is because of my concern for you that I am doing my job and this is the best I can be for you, John?
	As for feeling sorry or feeling stupid, that's just part of what comes up because of what we are doing here as we talk about things.
	It's important that you didn't hold back on this because it will have some meaning and it will shake out in a different way which we don't yet know.
John	Yeah, yeah … Um …
Susie	Let's meet next week as usual.
John	Yeah, OK, OK, we'll meet next week.
	I'm sorry, I mean I'm not sorry and I am sorry, you know what I mean.
	I – you know when I first came and I could hardly speak – *laugh* – and I was thinking if certain people could see me now they would be laughing so much. John in therapy, what a laugh, and I just didn't know what to say, I had not a clue and I hate – I didn't hate you but I thought, I just felt like you were a teacher, you know, and then I thought this morning on this sunny day, I thought my god, all these months and now I can't wait to get here and talk to you, and you always said – you were great because you didn't tell me off, and you didn't look impatient, you just said try to speak, try to tell, and I thought this morning well I will … and how wonderful that Susie has got

me to that place, but it's – well, I thought I would be walking out, I thought I might be walking out and skipping down the steps and …

Susie John, it would be a disservice to you, to send you out skipping down the steps because you woke up and you felt this and you shared it and then it all happened, because we are doing something that is about the rest of your life.

John Yeah.

Susie Uh-huh.

John Yeah.

Susie Alright, so I'll see you next week.

John Yeah, you are my life now but I'm not yours.

I don't mean to embarrass you, I'm stupid, I've slapped my wrist – *slapped wrist* – I'm not going to go down the river with you but you are very important to me and I'm glad I said what I did.

Susie John, I'll see you next week.

John Yes, thank you, bye now.

Susie Bye bye.

John walks out quite full. He's disappointed yes, but not only. I was surprised by the direction of this therapy session. Yet surprise is what keeps a therapist on her toes. We can never know what is coming because therapy is a subversive kind of conversation which can crackle with energy, or fear, despair or hope. We follow the feelings, the ideas, the tempo, the timbre of the patient's voice, finding ways of connecting even when we might, as in this instance with John, refuse what he wishes.

So much of therapy is involved in the view of disillusionment. We listen to what the person says, and how it is said and we put that together with our knowledge of how the individual is in the room with us. We don't so much pierce the bubble of their narrative but layer it, turn it inside out, look at it from unexpected perspectives, join it with what we know of how the individual has construed his or her circumstances. In this endeavour we move away from a picture of blame – my wife didn't understand me, my parents were cruel or negligent – to a more nuanced story of who they were in their psychological and social circumstances and their capacities.

The structures of class – as with John – also come into consideration, as do all the grand narratives which impact our world and the world of our parents and loved ones, to see how the individual mind, feelings, bodies and sense of self were forged in historic time and social attitudes. This moves us away from the view of the innocent and towards more complexity and a curiously enlightened disillusionment. This enlightening disillusionment enables the individual to be in a present without fantastical ideas about who they are or how hard done by they were. They can inhabit their history in new ways and have a richer present.

Afterword

The work of therapy is hidden and often invisible. People wonder what goes on in the room. Are therapists like the cabbie or hairdresser on to whom secrets are poured? Are we like the priest who hears confession? Does therapy create a dependent relationship? Is it all just psychobabble and self-justification? Is it a way of absolving oneself of guilt and responsibility?

As I hope I have shown, it is some of these things and none of them. In therapy, the opinions of the cabbie or hairdresser are absent. The quiet attention of the priest may be present but it is only the starting point. Dependency may exist for a period of time. Strange-sounding phrases may be intermittently developed between the therapy couple. Guilt and responsibility get taken out of their rigid boxes, examined and instead of being absolved, they may turn into other feelings or get reshaped.

Therapy, like any specialist work, can seem odd to an onlooker. It has been my aim as a psychotherapist when outside of the consulting room to show what is so fascinating and potentially life changing about the process and to apply the insights of therapy to the wider world.

I've wanted to show that therapy is a different way of talking and a different way of hearing. Therapy is as much a listening cure as it is a talking cure. The fact of being heard and of hearing one's words in a space in which they aren't necessarily interrupted or soothed but just hang, means they can reverberate. The individual (or the couple or the family) hears whether the words that have emerged are the right words. They are brought face to face with what lives inside of them but is hard to say. Like words chosen for a poem, the clutter of daily language is eviscerated. The words might need to be refined or they might shock the individual by being unexpected. Whatever they are, they carry a new weight.

Slips of the tongue of course can have significance but beyond that and in a more ordinary sense, one discovers, as one talks, the things that are difficult, the feelings that are rushed over, ignored or avoided. The words that resound, the silences, the ellipses, false starts, interruptions and hesitations which feature widely in the therapy, upend the conventions of ordinary conversation.

The patient, client, analysand (all unsatisfactory terms from my point of view and thus I tend to use them interchangeably) enters the room. How she or he does it, whether she looks at the therapist or down at the floor or smiles or uses the same opening words such as 'what a week', are all artefacts of the therapeutic encounter, as is the therapist's quiet welcome. Delight, a hug as a hello, a soothing arm around a back, common in friendship, are absent. In its place the therapist conveys an intense interest in seeing their client. Her or his ears, heart and body are open to what will unfold in the session, a session marked by time boundaries and usually occurring in the same place.

Therapy, psychoanalysis, is a collaborative venture. Two people

– analysand and analyst, patient or client and therapist – sit in a room together. It is a democratic process. The analysand initially drives the session because of what they bring and the way they set the conversation and the pace. As the relationship develops, the language that is created, the pauses, the reflections, the interjections of the therapist will be particular to each therapy relationship. The rules of therapy are there to create the conditions for the work of therapy to occur. They do not impose a similar shape or feel on each therapeutic couple.

I am not the same therapist with the six people we met in this book. Each one of them evokes differing aspects of me, uniquely draws on parts of my personality, taps on my heart strings with their own tune, or the tune I make inside of myself in relation to them. The way I feel about each of them is distinctive. What I offered was specific to them. Therapy is a bespoke craft with each therapeutic pair, or group, creating novel circumstances to respond to.

We met Louise and Richard, a couple on the cusp of parenthood. They came because a distance had opened up in their relationship. Richard seemed to have disappeared into his work as a builder and Louise, who had just taken a leave from her job as an events manager, felt abandoned and let down by Richard, a man she had adored until late in the pregnancy when the fact of the impending baby became obvious. Their need was for some rather urgent reconnecting with each other, albeit on different terms to the enchanted romance that enabled them to be carefree until recently.

They are both engaging individuals yet now disgruntled in

their own bubbles. It's hard, except, for brief moments, to feel what they have between them. Instead I felt Louise's urgency and Richard's reluctance. They pulled on me in opposing directions. I pondered whether the poles they express in the session we listened in on are important features of their relationship in general or specific to late pregnancy with its ensuing excitement and panic. I felt Louise's frustration and Richard's annoyance. I felt the tug between patience and impatience. I wanted Louise to back off so that Richard could take up some space but I'm aware of a dynamic between them that looks as though Richard will continue to retreat if Louise doesn't insist he participate in their new adventure. He needs her to beckon him.

Therapy is an emotional journey for the therapist, not just for her patients. Sometimes, as we saw, it's a high-wire act, as when John drops his unexpected bombshell. I'm on my toes, empathic and touched and trying to choreograph myself so that I don't puncture his dignity. Sometimes it calls for serenity and the simple wisdom of age as with Helen, the young woman lawyer, who has been in therapy for eighteen months. I remember the feelings she is so flummoxed by and feel the relief that I am no longer plagued with her questions. I want to convey that the questions and dilemmas she has are exciting but I need to be mindful that the experience of longevity can sound patronising, which is not what I feel. With Harriet, a school secretary in her forties, I was asked to understand the most painful of losses and feelings of helplessness. I believe I was helping her with those feelings but it will be a long haul and looking despair in the eye is not easy for either of us. With Jo, my compassion for her ineptitude mixes with exasperation as she unwittingly tests the boundaries of the therapeutic encounter whose conventions she does not yet know.

When I take someone on for therapy, I notice a somewhat peculiar process occurring inside me as I take a walk or as I'm doing the washing or am on my own in a non-work situation. Unprompted, I hear their speech pattern in my ear. Or my body spontaneously imitates the way they move, hold their head, smile or grimace and settle themselves in the therapy room. So with Jo, I heard where she placed the emphasis in a sentence and I felt myself take on her winsome smile as though to find a way to make a space inside of me for her.

When you offer yourself for therapy you can't know how long the person will stay with you but it could be for a considerable time. You are living their issues with them and there is a way in which the intimacy that evolves requires me to open myself, my body, my ears, my eyes, my sense of smell to fold them inside of me. Their idioms impact on me from the outside and the inside. I'm not simply a technician of the mind's tributaries. My analysands get into my own bloodstreams of thought, feeling and movement.

Each person who comes to therapy needs the same – to be listened to, to be thought about and to be heard in a private space – as well as something distinctive and personal. A harassed woman may require a sounding board to check that she isn't too critical of her children but it must be offered in such a way that she doesn't experience my responses as adding to her burden. Therapy needs to open some mental territory where she can think anew and afresh. A fifty-year-old man, sent to boarding school at seven when his parents divorced, wants me as an approving appreciative mother figure. I feel it, but I know we can't have me as an ideal replacement. The grief he feels for his early disillusionment and loss will not be healed by a better version of Mum, however seductive and cosy that feels.

A twenty-four-year-old young woman wants me to be a more distant version of her very capable but, from her perspective, slightly invasive mother. I have to see my own self as someone who can respond to what she needs without undermining her mother. The couple who need to see that the very things that annoy them in each other are the parts of themselves they like to disavow reminds me how a third person (the therapist) can tilt conversation to enable them to reknit their intimacy. The academically driven professor for whom emotions cause her difficulty has to be persuaded of the intellectual reasons for why emotions might be of value for her and why risking experiencing them with me will be useful. She likes to tussle and wants me to tussle back and I do. It's the way to reach her but it wouldn't suit many people. A man in an aggressive struggle with his stepson needs to know how his actions can have a positive outcome rather than a negative one. His reported conversations make me wretched inside, and the struggle to offer him an alternative puts me in a teacher situation.

Each individual who comes for help craves acceptance even though they may be diffident or even tetchy. Knowing that craving provides me with the motivation to get underneath and behind the cruelties and difficulties that I am hearing about, some of which will be thrown at me unexpectedly. How can I be useful? What am I being asked to do? Who am I a proxy for? What will enable my patient to clear the space around them and consider something from a different perspective? How can I parse their feelings so that they increase their emotional repertoire rather than repeatedly play the same no longer productive song?

Such are the demands of the consulting room and what gets stirred up in the therapist.

The psychoanalytic session always has had a strong aesthetic for me. It is a practice like the work of painting or writing or composing or dancing or working on a scientific problem. It requires knowledge which constantly refreshes itself. It requires expertise and it requires an ear to shape, feel and touch the heart of the issues so that they can be revisioned. At the same time there is a physical aesthetic, by which I mean the resonance and rhythm of a session, how noisy it is, the weight of the silences, the relationship between therapeutic dialogue and reflectiveness, the way the bodies in the room move forward and back into the shared space in response to intensity.

In Richard and Louise's session I felt an urgency to quiet the noise. I wanted to clear the jangle in my ears and slow the language into a different register. The jangle I experienced is an unthought-out signal that the contact between them needed reshaping.

What constitutes the aesthetic of psychoanalytic therapy is harder to pin down. The aesthetic is not to do with harmony, because it can be decidedly unharmonious. I think it is probably to do with the struggle for truth. A provisional truth to be sure, but an honesty to engage in a venture which presents itself like a mess of rubbish, with no coherence except for its capacity to make the individual feel helpless and hopeless. Through a process of clearing and examining, what needs repairing, what needs sorting, what needs protecting, what needs discarding, what needs nurturing, and in what order these things can be done, constitutes an aesthetic. Marked by rhythm and timbre, by the idiom established in each analyst-analysand couple and by the pacing, something beautiful evolves at both a psychological and spiritual level.

Therapy is a deep practice. It searches for veracity. One truth can open to another which may shade what is first understood. The intricate constructions of the human mind shift during the course of therapy. Being a participant observer to the changing of internal structures and of the expansion of feelings is very satisfying. Seeing how defences are used, and how they can be worked around and in time dissolve, has a beauty which is perhaps akin to the mathematician or physicist's experience of finding an equation elegant.

I find the particulars of learning how an individual's internal world works fascinating. We are always learning. We all split parts of experience off. We all forget. We all protect ourselves against certain ideas and feelings. We do this because if we remembered and felt everything there wouldn't be much psychic space for the present. While psychoanalysts theorise our ways of understanding mind management, the work of brain scientists and neuropsychologists is dovetailing with what we discover in the consulting room. As we understand the compelling nature of the pull to repeat what may ill serve us, so the neuroscientists are attempting to plot the ways in which the mind prunes and shapes experience through repeated actions and beliefs. All three disciplines confirm the evidence that the essence of the human is the consequence of our long learning outside the womb. We don't arrive knowing how to walk and talk and think and feel. We apprehend how to do so in the context of the relationships which receive us. Those relationships, embedded in time and place and economic circumstances, then structure our mind, our feelings, our brains, our desires, our behaviours and the way we are embodied.

Therapy takes so very long because the structures of mind we develop in infancy, childhood and adolescence are quasi-material structures. They are who we are and although the human mind and brain have great plasticity, desired change can be very difficult. Psychoanalytic therapy, with its emphasis on looking behind our defence structures to the beliefs and feelings that can appear dangerous or unknown, involves the therapist serving as an external anchor (hence the caricature of being overly dependent on the analyst) while the work of deconstructing and reconstructing follows. In therapy you don't just learn a new language to add to your repertoire, you relinquish unhelpful parts of the mother tongue and weave them together with the knowledge of a new grammar. The curiosity a therapist has towards the analysand's structures designate us as anthropologists of the mind. Each individual mind embodies complex understandings of social relationships – the interplay between self – what is allowed and what is sequestered and what to do with what isn't allowed. To know an individual is to know some of their time in history, in place, in class, gender, caste, race and the society and family constellation they have emerged from. An individual is the outcome of her engagement with others from birth (and some would argue, the womb) onwards.

As we unlearn and remake so we impact on those we are close with. We all know this in a matter-of-fact way: a bully can intimidate. An easy, confident person can make us feel included and capable. A puffed-up show-off can make us feel competitive. Our minds are both resilient and flexible. We can explain Stockholm Syndrome or the affection built up for an abuser by the mind's capacity to make accommodations to need. In therapy, however, the way one mind has an impact on another becomes part of the subject of the therapy. This makes for an intensity and truth-seeking which forms part of the aesthetic.

So what difference does therapy make? Why should someone come? Does everyone need to come?

Many live with painful family secrets which can erupt at Christmas or when the family gets together. Many live with unease or are beset by symptoms that intensify. Many feel an emptiness or a confusion about why they can't activate their desires, or why they sabotage the things they imagine they want. For others, their relationships stall, unravel and devastate them and they don't know why. Richard, Louise, Harriet, Helen, Jo and John were in difficulty. That's why they came. Talking with family and friends had not reached the places that could help them sufficiently. John tells movingly of the aliveness that he now feels as though before he was walking through life not living it. He's not alive because he's fallen for me. He's alive because he's fallen for himself. Yes, love can look like the catalyst but a more important catalyst was my being deeply interested in him. He found a way to open himself up. He began to see himself as being of value; to himself and to me. The negative self-image he carried didn't just dissolve. He'd had to work hard not to slot the attention he's been receiving into a set of categories that nullified it; 'she's just doing her job' (true but nevertheless what makes for the healing). Or, 'if I show her it is affecting me, she'll have power over me', and he had to risk being vulnerable to me in order to change himself inside.

Love of course does do that – temporarily. It allows us to see ourselves differently because we are loved and do love, but if love itself isn't sufficient for change, because the patterns that hurt can be stimulated in a new relationship, then therapy can be of profound help.

With Harriet, therapy is about addressing a present wound that has activated a previous loss that ruptured everything she knew about life. She didn't just lose her father, she lost her mother too because despite her mother being with her, she was divorced from her own home and community. The bereft mother conveyed a resigned attitude about getting on with life which left a depressive hole in Harriet which she coped with well enough until the failures of the IVF and her own flight from her partner. Harriet's present loss is allowing her to face the earlier loss from which she cut off as she turned herself into the nice girl who could try to fit in. Her earlier depressive disposition will clear. It will become reconstituted as a loss and that will restore something that she's been missing without knowing it.

Listening to Helen, we hear her desire to understand the meaning of life. It's a big question which will be made up of many small answers. When I say that we are working to rearrange Helen's internal furniture, I mean that the structures of her psyche need to be reorganised so that she can discover what she wants and join it up with an emerging Helen inside of herself. Such changes won't be easily integrated in the first instance. They may involve reconsidering her job, her boyfriend, her relationship to her parents and her interests as she struggles to expand herself from the inside out and not through her accoutrements. Doing so will give her a life of meaning. It won't be without sadness, sorrow or disappointment, for those are parts of life but she will have embodied Freud's famous dictum, to move from hysteria to ordinary human unhappiness.

Jo presented us with a different dilemma. She came because her friend had told her to. She's lost. Her acting different roles gave her ways to imagine and play a life but not enough grounding to find truths for herself. Her bubbly pleasing persona is shielding a more desperate stance which therapy will be able to address – should she let it – so that she can stop bobbing around and find what she needs to know about herself in future.

Richard and Louise have some readjusting to do. Becoming parents is an opportunity for each of them to create a present rather than repeat their history and the history of their parents. And this is a salient fact of therapy, that history can be in the past rather than unknowingly casting its pall over the present. The past acknowledged allows for a richer, layered and less fearful present.

But I haven't answered the question of whether therapy is for everyone. For me the answer is no. Therapy is one kind of vector into that wonderful adventure, an examined life. It is an intimate and delicate route but makes little sense unless one is in psychological trouble. Yes, we can all benefit from becoming emotionally literate, and social programmes which help expectant parents, educators, doctors, nurses and so on expand their own emotional knowledge are effective ways to enable us to know ourselves, to connect well with other(s) and be alright in our own skin.

For others, art, literature, bonding through sport, political or spiritual activity, satisfying enough work and so on, will provide meaning. But it is an arduous struggle in a time of political cruelty which wreaks extreme economic and social division, while despoiling our environment and creating divisions inside of us.

Many live lives of quiet desperation, as David Henry Thoreau told us in *Walden*. Therapy cannot answer these ills on its own. Psychoanalytic ways of thinking have much to bring to public policy and the political conversation, whether about the family, child development, bonding, body image, emotional collapse, unwanted teenage pregnancy, repeat offenders, gangs, violent or abusive relationships, attachment difficulties, compulsive eating (or not eating), smoking and cutting, alienation, war, fears of immigrants and so on.

Like other disciplines such as sociology, economics and social psychology, psychoanalytic thinking should have a place at public policy tables as its insights speak to the mismatch between people's inner and outer experience – the gap between what they say and what they feel, which no other discipline addresses. Psychoanalysis studies people in the process of change, illuminating unexpected reasons and motivations, which, if understood, could lead policy-makers to different emphases as they try to affect wanted social change. In this sense psychoanalytic thinking, as a technocratic discipline, has something to bring to the table alongside other analytic methods, not in the way of behavioral economics with its notion of nudge. Psychoanalytic prompts are in a sense anti-directive and thus expansive. It can never supplant other forms of research but it can enrich them.

Symptoms of distress in our society are exacerbated by changes in global culture and the development of rampant consumer-ism which is itself a pointer to the horrors of ordinary needs for connection and contribution not met. We are invited to partici-pate in society by taking up identity markers such as brands and viewing ourselves as a brand. A sense of belonging is fostered by purchasing but its falsity fails to satisfy. So, too, are funda-mentalist modes of thought, whether they are xenophobias, nationalisms, racisms or gender hatreds. In fundamental-ist modes of thought, only a narrow band of feelings can be tolerated and solutions to injustices are expressed through adherence to political, sectarian or religious party lines which have a hard time with complexity. They abhor internal dissent while thriving on external disagreement. What consumerism and fundamentalism both highlight is the human desperation to belong. This is not pathological; the desperation to belong is what makes us human. When we belong we can feel safe being separate. If we can't, the expression we find for it when it goes awry can be deadly.

So therapy for everyone? Again, I say no. But therapeutic ideas to enter social discourse, I say yes. We don't and can't fully know ourselves. That is a conceit to protect us from feeling vulnerable and helpless. Much of what we do and how we go about it is unconscious. Therapeutic ideas can't make us fully conscious but they can make us less arrogant and more humble in a generous manner about what it means to be human and to live.

Acknowledgements

My thanks:

To Sinead Matthews, Noo Kirby, Noma Dumezweni, Peter Wright, Liz White and Nat Martello White, the superb actors.

To Ian Rickson and Kevin Dawson for such an enjoyable working relationship. To Gareth Isles for sound engineering that really works.

To Gudrun Wiborg, Luise Eichenbaum, Brett Kahr, Caroline Pick, Sally Berry, Jane Haberlin, Gillian Slovo, Kamila Shamsie, Sian Putnam and Barbara Nettleton.

And to Penny Daniel and Andrew Franklin, my lovely and very capable editor and publisher.